Sunset

Bonsai

by Susan Lang and the Editors of Sunset Books

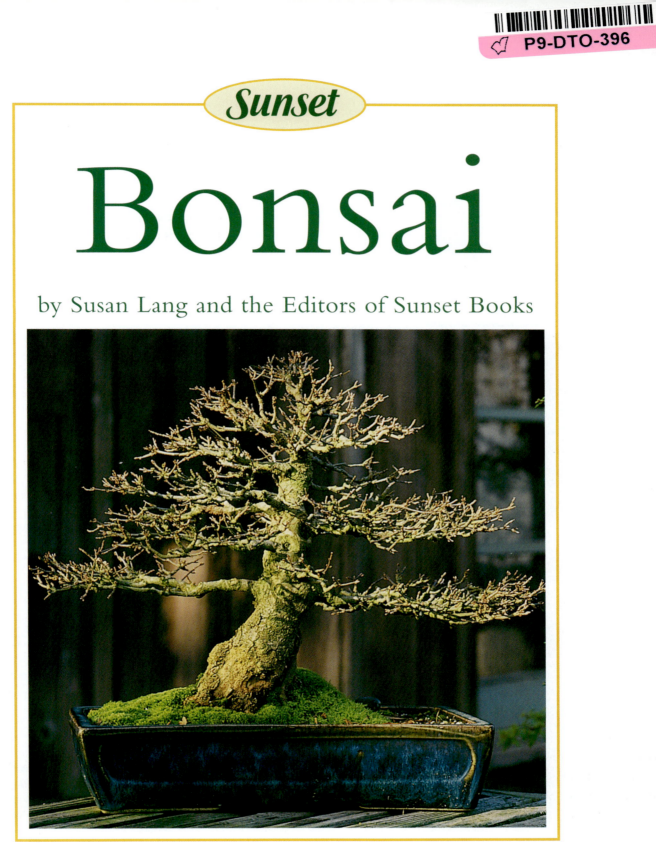

Menlo Park, California

Small Is Big

The popularity of bonsai is on the rise, as more and more people around the world discover fulfillment in the hobby. Countless clubs and societies are venues for devotees to get together with other bonsai enthusiasts and share their knowledge with newcomers.

Whether you participate in a group or work on your own, this book will be an indispensable guide to training and caring for bonsai. The techniques shown here are arranged by degree of difficulty, creating an easy-to-follow path from the beginning to the intermediate and more advanced levels.

We gratefully acknowledge Dennis Makishima for demonstrating the techniques in the photo sequences, as well as providing invaluable counsel and reviewing the manuscript. Thanks also to David DeGroot, Doris Froning, Mas Imazumi, Hideko Metaxas, Yvonne Padilla, Ed Trout, Terry Ward, and Jack Wikle for their assistance and advice.

SUNSET BOOKS

Vice President, General Manager: Richard A. Smeby
Vice President, Editorial Director: Bob Doyle
Production Director: Lory Day
Director of Operations: Rosann Sutherland
Sales Development Director: Linda Barker
Art Director: Vasken Guiragossian

STAFF FOR THIS BOOK

Managing Editor: Susan Bryant Caron
Writer: Susan Lang
Sunset Books Senior Editor: Marianne Lipanovich
Copy Editor: Julie Harris
Illustrator: Rik Olson
Principal Photographer: Saxon Holt
Map Design and Cartography: Reineck & Reineck, San Francisco
Additional Page Production: Linda M. Bouchard
Production Coordinator: Eligio Hernandez
Proofreader: Alicia Eckley

Cover: Azalea (*Rhododendron*) photography by Saxon Holt. False cypress (*Chamaecyparis*) border photography by Marion Brenner.

10 9 8 7 6 5 4 3 2 1

First printing January 2003

For additional copies of *Bonsai* or any other Sunset book, call 1-800-526-5111 or visit us at *www.sunsetbooks.com*

Additional Photographers: **Peter L. Bloomer:** 8, 53T, 102B, 108B, 118B; **Peter L. Bloomer–Bonsai Clubs International:** 100T, 103T, 118T; **Peter L. Bloomer–U.S. National Bonsai Collection Courtesy National Bonsai Foundation U.S. National Arboretum Washington, DC:** 6B, 7T, 9L, 10T, 53B, 68, 84, 85, 101TR, 104T, 106TL, 106TR, 117B, 119TL, 122R; **Kathleen Norris Brenzel:** 102T; **David DeGroot:** 11, 33, 65, 83, 116T; **Alan & Linda Detrick:** 67T; **John Edwards:** 7BL, 7BR, 13L, 13BR, 18L, 95, 113B; **Allan Mandell:** 94BL, 94BR; **Charles Mann:** 60B; **David McDonald/PhotoGarden, Inc.:** 120L, 121BR; **Jerry Pavia:** 104B, 105TL, 107T, 109L, 113T, 115B, 117T, 119TR; **Michael S. Thompson:** 13TR, 105B, 108R, 110T, 111B; **Michael S. Thompson © Pacific Rim Bonsai Collection:** 121BL; **Ed Trout:** 52, 102R, 115T; **William Valavanis:** 19, 32B, 80, 105TR, 111TR, 112T; **Weyerhaeuser Company © Pacific Rim Bonsai Collection:** 9R, 15, 104L, 108T, 112B, 113R, 116R, 120B, 122L; **Bob Wigand:** 96T, 101TL, 101B, 106B, 107B, 109R, 110B.

contents

CHAPTER ONE

An Ancient Art

AN ASIAN TRADITION *whose roots can be traced back more than a thousand years, bonsai combines the aesthetics of fine art with the skills of horticulture. What originated as an exotic art form has spread beyond the Far East and captured the fancy of cultures throughout the world. To the uninitiated, bonsai may appear simply to be the cultivation of dwarfed plants. But rather than produce a miniature replica of a tree faithful in every detail, a true bonsai artist evokes the spirit of nature, much as a painter or sculptor evokes a mood or a sense of place. To many, bonsai represents the very essence of the natural world. In this book, you will enter the beguiling world of bonsai—discovering the rich history, getting a feel for what constitutes a satisfying specimen, and learning the fundamentals of the art.*

What Is Bonsai?

It's easy to assume that bonsai consists simply of growing a miniature tree in a small container—but nothing could be further from the truth. A fine bonsai is actually an artistic representation of nature in microcosm.

NO ORDINARY POTTED PLANT

The term "bonsai" (pronounced bone-sigh) combines two Japanese words, *bon* meaning tray and *sai* meaning to create. Thus, thinking of a bonsai as a mere potted plant, even a dwarfed one, doesn't do it justice. Artistry is so much a part of bonsai that the Japanese have a different term, *hachi-no-ki*, for an ordinary potted plant.

Although the art form is often equated with copying nature, a well-executed bonsai is actually its creator's vision of nature. Because bonsai are intended to be evocative statements rather than exact reproductions, they have an artistic kinship with the impressionist school of painting. An impressionist painter uses brushwork to suggest rather than to depict realistically. The result draws the viewer into the picture and stimulates the imagination to interact with it.

In bonsai the sweep of a branch may suggest a seaside cliff with waves crashing below. The deliberately weathered branches of a gnarled conifer may evoke the thin mountain air at timberline. A downward-growing trunk may hint at a waterfall. When you view a bonsai, you see an abstraction of nature and respond to it.

A CREATIVE JOURNEY

Patience is a virtue; a bonsai is not made overnight. A plant spends several years in a training phase before it merits the name "bonsai." And even then the

TOP: *This Colorado blue spruce* (Picea pungens glauca) *is a bonsai-in-training. It will eventually end up with fewer branches and a smaller, shallower pot.*

LEFT: *A mature bonsai, this Japanese red pine* (Pinus densiflora) *has been fully developed.*

creation is not complete, for the tree will undergo further refinement. Just how long it takes to finish a bonsai depends on when the person who created it feels that it is finished—or rather when he or she has done everything to develop the plant's essence. In a way, the work is never finished because the medium is alive and will continue to grow.

In bonsai the creative journey is as important as the finished product. It doesn't matter whether the bonsai becomes a masterwork displayed in a museum or a piece of art that provides deep satisfaction to just the person who created it. That so much personal fulfillment can be derived from bonsai, regardless of a hobbyist's level of proficiency, explains in part why the art form attracts so many devotees who throw themselves wholeheartedly into it.

*A lightning strike is suggested by the apex of the foemina juniper (*Juniperus chinensis *'Foemina') shown at right. The bonsai artist artificially created deadwood to tell the tale of the tree's struggle against nature.*

*Even a mature bonsai may change dramatically to satisfy an artist's evolving vision. The photo at immediate right shows a shimpaku juniper (*Juniperus chinensis sargentii) *before its tip was shortened and fuller foliage pads were developed for a more contemporary look. The photo at far right shows the transformed juniper five years later.*

Evolution of an Art

Although bonsai was introduced to the West from Japan and much of the terminology is Japanese, the first record actually comes from China. These two countries have had the greatest impact on bonsai practiced here, although a North American version has begun to emerge. Recently, some Japanese bonsai masters have veered from the classic to the contemporary and exported their vision. Today, both traditional and modern approaches attract devotees.

A miniature landscape containing mountains and water, and a boat for scale, is in the Chinese tradition.

CHINESE BEGINNINGS

The earliest evidence of bonsai as an art form is found in Chinese frescoes dating back to A.D. 220. They clearly show floral bonsai (what we would think of as flower arrangements) in complementary containers. The first depiction of bonsai plants rather than flowers comes from Tang dynasty tomb murals dating from A.D. 760, although the practice of cultivating such plants is thought to have existed before the start of the Eastern Jin dynasty in A.D. 317.

Bonsai (called *penjing* in China) flourished during subsequent dynasties, and various schools of bonsai art evolved. Individual specimens, often elaborately contorted, became one form of expression. Another was the "landscape bonsai," in which dwarfed plants were combined in shallow trays with rocks to represent mountains, water to depict lakes and rivers, and miniature structures to lend scale.

FROM CHINA TO JAPAN

Initial contact between China and Japan occurred around 200 B.C., but it was not until the Tang dynasty (A.D. 618–906) that a Japanese cultural delegation traveled to China and was almost certainly exposed to bonsai. The earliest pictorial record of bonsai in Japan is on a scroll dating to 1185. By the first half of the 14th century, "bonsai" made its appearance in Japanese writing.

For hundreds of years, Japanese practitioners built upon Chinese

The bald cypress (Taxodium distichum) *at left was given an upright shape in the traditional Japanese model, while the same species above was styled more naturally.*

styles. Gradually the Japanese approach diverged from the Chinese as bonsai artists began to seek out wild plants that had been artfully altered by the elements. Naturally dwarfed trees that had been weathered into unusual shapes became highly prized, spurring vast collections.

When good plants became hard to find, bonsai artists replicated nature's handiwork by skillfully training domestic plants. In the mid-19th century, training methods for creating bonsai specimens were refined, and the aesthetic principles of Japanese bonsai as they exist today were codified.

TO THE WESTERN WORLD

As a result of Chinese and Japanese policies of isolation, Westerners had little knowledge of bonsai until the beginning of the 20th century. Records show that in 1907, Windsor Castle had a bonsai collection. And the public response to bonsai displays at a London exhibition in 1909 was enthusiastic.

The first serious bonsai practitioners on this continent were Japanese immigrants who settled on the West Coast in the early 20th century. Most were sent to internment camps during World War II. Afterward, the majority returned West, where the main jobs available to them were in farming, plant propagation, or gardening. A close connection with plants resulted in many taking up bonsai as a hobby. Because of their heritage, they followed the classic Japanese model and taught it to others.

Many U.S. servicemen stationed in Japan after the war also returned with enthusiasm for the Japanese version of bonsai, as have North Americans traveling

to Japan in more recent decades. By comparison, Chinese models of bonsai were late to arrive because of minimal contact between China and the West after the 1949 Chinese Revolution.

BONSAI TODAY

Although the traditional Japanese model still predominates in North America, bonsai here is fast becoming a mosaic of different schools and styles.

The many species of fig (Ficus) are popular subjects for tropical bonsai. The aerial roots and umbrella-shaped crown of this specimen give it a naturalistic appearance.

Bonsai Classification

Bonsai is an art of endless variety: each specimen is an individual. Nonetheless, all plants can be classified in two ways—by size and basic design style.

SIZE *Mature bonsai can range from a few inches to about 4 feet in height. Today bonsai are often separated into two categories:* shohin *for plants up to 8 inches tall, and* bonsai *for specimens 8 inches or taller. Historically, though, size has been subdivided into five categories:*

Miniature	under 4"
Small	4 to 8"
Medium	8 to 24"
Large	24 to 36"
Extra-large	36 to 48"

Small and medium specimens are most common. It's more difficult to do fine detail work on miniature bonsai, and the sheer bulk of large specimens makes them cumbersome.

STYLE *The many shapes of bonsai are actually variations on basic,*

well-defined styles. When you look beyond the specimen differences, you will notice a number of general themes.

Many broad bonsai style categories are defined by trunk formation—whether the trunk is straight, curved, slanted, or cascading. The majority of trunk-based styles feature plants with a single trunk. The character of branches determines other styles. Still other styles are based on root configuration or on a total composition.

Subsequent chapters offer details on various styles. The five basic Japanese styles—formal upright, informal upright, slanting, semicascade, and cascade—are described in the chapter beginning on page 35. Those requiring more expertise—broom, windswept, weeping, multitrunk, grove, and raft—are discussed in the chapter that begins on page 57. For the most challenging—literati, exposed root, root over rock, driftwood, and hollow trunk—turn to the chapter starting on page 75.

Extra-large and miniature, they're both bonsai. A burly coast live oak (Quercus agrifolia) shelters a tiny plant of Serissa foetida trained in similar fashion.

Tropical looks from such warm-weather locales as Hawaii, southern Florida, and Puerto Rico are now a big part of the picture. Far from being confined to hot spots, this form of bonsai also enjoys great popularity in wintry climes because many of the species used can be cultivated indoors. Some proponents prefer to style all tropical plants naturally; others follow the Japanese model for some specimens. (For more information on tropical bonsai, see pages 52–53.)

Many bonsai hobbyists growing temperate plants also take cues from nature rather than follow traditional styles. The live oak model has emerged as a bonsai style in California and other places where these trees grow. In New Orleans, the bald cypress is often given the kind of flat top and open, spreading canopy seen in mature specimens in nature instead of a rigidly upright shape in the classic Japanese model (see the photos on page 9).

Influences have crept in from China, Vietnam,

Korea, and other parts of Asia. Even Japan offers a new, contemporary version of bonsai, often described as highly stylized or even abstract. Its advocates feel it better expresses the artist's vision, while those who prefer the classic form say that the trees look less natural.

In traditional Japanese bonsai the trunk and major branches are wired to train growth in specific directions; in the newer form all branches and even small twigs are wired, down to the tip. In the older style, deadwood is fairly rough, while in the contemporary style it is smoother and more polished. The new

approach also features dramatically carved wood (special power tools were designed for carving), a fuller foliage head on conifers, unconventionally shaped pots, and more colorful containers for deciduous trees.

In less than a century, bonsai has become an internationally practiced art, rooted in the Japanese tradition but keeping pace with modern developments. How to explain such widespread interest? Maybe it's just difficult to resist a pastime combining art, history, and gardening in a process that instills a sense of tranquility and creates an object of beauty.

This dramatic shimpaku juniper (Juniperus chinensis sargentii) *epitomizes the contemporary form of bonsai. Deadwood is a sculptural feature that counterbalances a dense, finely detailed foliage head.*

Learning More About Bonsai

Joining a club is one of the best ways to step more confidently into the world of bonsai. Organizations abound, many offering workshops. Local bonsai shows offer a particularly good chance to glean advice from other enthusiasts. The Internet is another good source of information; just enter the word "bonsai" into a search engine for a list of potentially informative Web sites. For inspiration visit some of the permanent collections listed below, if you're in the vicinity.

BONSAI SOCIETIES

The following are some of the major bonsai associations offering a full range of activities; they can also direct you to clubs in your area. Note that the mailing address may change depending on who handles membership registration. Check the group's Web site for up-to-date information and links to other bonsai groups and services.

AMERICAN BONSAI SOCIETY
P.O. Box 351604
Toledo, OH 43635
www.absbonsai.org

BONSAI CLUBS INTERNATIONAL
P.O. Box 8445
Metairie, LA 70011
www.bonsai-bci.com

GOLDEN STATE BONSAI FEDERATION
P.O. Box 1746
Pollock Pines, CA 95726
www.gsbf-bonsai.org

PUBLIC COLLECTIONS

Permanent collections of fine-quality bonsai offer another valuable resource for newcomers to the bonsai world as well as for practitioners of all levels. The following are among the finest collections in North America.

BROOKLYN BOTANIC GARDEN
C.V. Starr Bonsai Museum
1000 Washington Ave.
Brooklyn, NY 11225
(718) 623-7200
*www.bbg.org/exp/stroll/
conservatory_bonsai.html*

GOLDEN STATE BONSAI FEDERATION
Golden State Bonsai Collection–North
666 Bellevue Ave./Lake Merritt
Oakland, CA 94610
(510) 763-8409
www.gsbf-bonsai.org/collectionnorth

Golden State Bonsai Collection at
    the Huntington
Huntington Library, Art Collections,
    and Botanical Gardens
1151 Oxford Rd.
San Marino, CA 91108
(626) 405-2100
*www.huntington.org/BotanicalDiv/
JapanGard.html*

MONTRÉAL BOTANICAL GARDEN
(JARDIN BOTANIQUE DE MONTRÉAL)
4101 Sherbrooke East
Montréal, Québec, Canada H1X 2B2
(514) 872-1400
*www2.ville.montreal.qc.ca/jardin/en/
japonais/bonsais.htm*

MORIKAMI MUSEUM AND
JAPANESE GARDENS
4000 Morikami Park Rd.
Delray Beach, FL 33444
(561) 495-0233
www.morikami.org/home.html

PACIFIC RIM BONSAI COLLECTION
Weyerhaeuser Corporate Campus
33663 Weyerhaeuser Way South
Federal Way, WA 98003
(253) 924-5206
www.weyerhaeuser.com/bonsai

U.S. NATIONAL ARBORETUM
The National Bonsai and
    Penjing Museum
3501 New York Ave. NE
Washington, DC 20002
(202) 245-2726
www.bonsai-nbf.org

Dozens of fine bonsai are exhibited at the Golden State Bonsai Federation collection in Oakland, California. The Japanese-style garden was designed especially to showcase the bonsai.

Design Considerations

A basic knowledge of plant care is essential in bonsai. But visualizing just how you want a plant to look—and determining how best to achieve that result—calls for artistry. Part of the pleasure of bonsai is cultivating your own artistic sensibility.

Natural trees are models for bonsai. At left, pines in a natural grove illustrate how trunks are tall and slender when trees are clustered. At right, surface roots often snake in intriguing patterns, as on this fig (Ficus).

A study of well-executed bonsai illustrates how natural growth patterns can be translated into a small plant in a pot. Bonsai exhibits offer good opportunities for three-dimensional views of plants and close-ups of trunks, branches, foliage, and roots.

THE APPEARANCE OF AGE

When you look at bonsai, you'll notice something beyond the obvious fact that these plants are small. Except for young bonsai-in-training, most specimens seem much older than their diminutive size suggests. They may also appear to be veterans of years of struggle against natural forces that have significantly altered their forms. Indeed, in some carefully tended specimens the flame of life may appear to be barely flickering.

While it's true that you'll see bonsai specimens older than you are (in exceptional cases, even

DEVELOPING AN EYE

To develop a sense of natural design—an important step since a well-conceived bonsai evokes the essence of nature—study trees growing in the wild. Observe how they grow differently in response to weather, topography, and soil conditions.

Learn to recognize the conditions that make a tree grow in a particular manner. Trees tend to lean toward water and lowland and away from the wind. A tree's trunk may be twisted or even prostrate in harsh growing

conditions, but staunchly upright in a more protected spot. On a rocky foundation, large surface roots may clasp the rock or snake toward the soil.

Foliage grows where it gets maximum sunlight. Trees clustered in tight groves bear most of their leaves at the top of the shared canopy. They grow straight and tall, their branches often reaching upward rather than outward. Trees that are not crowded together tend to spread their branches more widely and bear a full canopy of foliage.

Flaking bark and well-developed foliage pads give Juniperus procumbens *'Nana', a dwarf ground cover juniper, the look of age.*

PLEASING PROPORTIONS
In the multitrunked example at far left, a large root has given rise to an overlarge trunk terminating in a bulky foliage pad. The result is a sense of disharmony. A smaller root, more slender trunk, and smaller foliage pad, as shown at immediate left, improve the composition. The largest-diameter trunk is the tallest, with the largest top; the medium one is next in height, with a medium-size top; and the thinnest one is the shortest, with the smallest top.

older than several generations of your family), not all good bonsai plants are old. Many specimens are products of the human hand working with nature to produce the appearance of age.

ARTISTIC UNITY

All parts of a bonsai—roots, trunk, branches, and foliage—must make a pleasing whole if the specimen is to appear unified. Artistic concepts of balance, proportion, line, and form all come into play, even if they are not always conscious considerations. Bonsai practitioners often make intuitive adjustments until they are satisfied. When all the elements are harmoniously integrated, the result is convincing. If they are slighted, the specimen will be uninspiring at best.

BALANCE AND PROPORTION The location of branches and foliage, variety in branch sizes, and placement of the plant in the pot all contribute to creating balance

and proportion that are pleasing to the eye.

Balance doesn't dictate symmetry: you'll seldom find a perfectly symmetrical bonsai. Instead, balance refers to distribution—a heavy branch on one side balanced by a curve on the other, for example.

Proportion refers to the relative sizes of a plant's elements. If, for instance, a branch on one side is too massive for its counterbalance, it will seem out of proportion.

LINE AND FORM The line of a bonsai composition is determined

by the movement or flow of the trunk and by the relationship of the plant's apex (growing tip) to the trunk base. Is the apex directly above the base or at an angle from it? Or does it fall below the container?

Form, or outline, refers to how you flesh out the line. In classic Japanese bonsai, the form resembles an irregular triangle (see "Rule of Three" below). Within the triangle, you decide on the amount and delicacy of branching, foliage density, and other elements of the composition.

RULE OF THREE
Traditional Japanese bonsai design is based on the "rule of three," which depicts earth, man, and heaven in the form of an asymmetrical triangle. The lowest and farthest-reaching branch tip is considered the lowest point (earth), the apex of the plant is the highest point (heaven), and the foliage tip on the side opposite the lowest point is the midpoint (man).

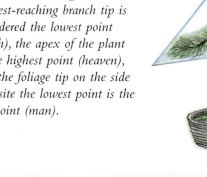

Bonsai for Seasonal Interest

Bonsai practitioners often punctuate their collections of predominately evergreen bonsai with specimens that offer seasonal appeal. Few bonsai undergo more spectacular transformations through the year than crabapple *(Malus)*. The specimen shown here offers the ultimate in seasonal interest: flowers in spring, lush foliage and developing fruit in summer, colorful leaves and ripe fruit in autumn, and persistent fruit on leafless branches in winter.

Deciduous trees that are grown for foliage rather than flowers or fruit are among the other bonsai plants that change their appearance with the seasons. For example, a maidenhair tree *(Ginkgo biloba)* has fresh green summer foliage that turns bright yellow in fall, then drops to reveal a lovely winter silhouette. So popular are deciduous trees that many bonsai clubs hold exhibits that feature just winter silhouettes.

SPRING

SUMMER

FALL

WINTER

Applying Design Principles

Good design can't be expressed in a set of absolute rules. If it could, all bonsai would look much alike. But there are some general artistic principles to consider in creating a pleasing bonsai. These precepts cover all parts of the plant—trunk, branches, foliage, and roots—as well as the direction from which you view it, and the container in which it grows.

TRUNK

Although no one part of a bonsai is more important than another, the trunk's structure is central to its style. A thick trunk suggests a mature tree, whether or not it is actually old, but if a trunk is too thick, it merely appears to be out of proportion. An old rule of thumb states that the height of the bonsai should be roughly six times the width of the trunk's base. However, an inspection of fine bonsai will reveal that many specimens are taller—and pleasingly so.

A trunk should taper gracefully and naturally to its terminal point. A cylindrical trunk (with the same thickness at the top and bottom) makes the bonsai look more like a telephone pole than a tree. For this reason, you can't just lop off a trunk to create an apex at a suitable height. You'll need to train the uppermost branch into a vertical position to continue the trunk's line and taper, or allow the stump to sprout and then train one of the shoots as the new top.

Some bonsai practitioners advise keeping trunk curves to a minimum and avoiding abrupt bends. Others believe that guideline is overstated; they argue that gentle curves can convey a feeling of grace, and strong ones a sense of drama. Depending on the style you want, a few bends may be pleasing, while too many may distract and appear artificial. A well-developed aesthetic sense is the only way to tell if you've gone too far, or not far enough.

A trunk scarred from wiring or bad pruning is seldom admired, but one that appears aged, even weather-beaten, is cherished. As a bonsai matures, its trunk will look more venerable. You can also add age by such techniques as stripping off bark; see pages 70–71.

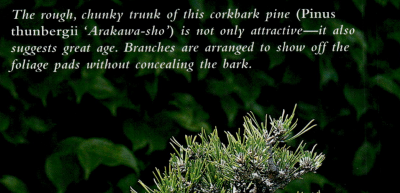

The rough, chunky trunk of this corkbark pine (Pinus thunbergii *'Arakawa-sho')* *is not only attractive—it also suggests great age. Branches are arranged to show off the foliage pads without concealing the bark.*

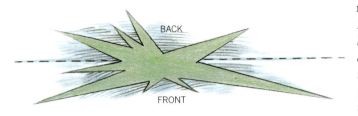

BACK

FRONT

BRANCHING PATTERN
In a well-conceived bonsai, branches vary in diameter and length and have ample space between them. Many branches, especially the bottom two and some smaller ones near the top, angle slightly forward. None point directly at the viewer (such branches are jokingly referred to as "eye pokers") or directly to the back.

BRANCHES

Left to their own devices, trees often branch heavily and randomly. Most bonsai, in contrast, have relatively few branches, and these are carefully spaced and directed. The branching pattern establishes the outline of the bonsai, shows the trunk to best advantage, and creates depth of field.

DIMENSIONS To maintain proper proportion, branches should be conspicuously smaller in diameter than the trunk. Generally, thicker branches should appear on the lower part of the tree, and progressively finer branches higher up the tree. Spaces between branches should vary, gradually diminishing toward the plant's apex.

Branches should also vary in length. You might think that having the lowest branch long, the one above it shorter, and the next one shorter still would create the desired effect, but such a rigid gradation can produce an overly stiff, artificial effect.

An oft-quoted guideline states that the combined length of the two longest branches (usually the lowest ones) should equal about half the height of the bonsai. But there are many exceptions. If, for instance, you have a short plant with a thick trunk, the combined length of the bonsai's two longest branches might actually be greater than its height. Rather than using a mathematical formula, what works better is to have a tree taller than wide or vice versa.

RAMIFICATION Good ramification—twigginess—suggests maturity. The idea is to develop finer and finer growth toward the ends of the branches. Each branch should taper toward a point at the tip. Lateral branches should grow in the same plane as the parent limb.

ANGLE OF SLOPE In many of the most pleasing bonsai, the angle of slope is roughly the same for all branches. The branches of many needle-leafed evergreens in nature may point upward when young but angle downward in maturity. Bonsai artists often train all branches on such trees downward to create the impression of age.

DEPTH Branches at the back of the tree will keep a bonsai from looking two-dimensional. Such branches also create a backdrop of smaller limbs and foliage against which the bonsai's forward structure is displayed. The branches should be short and angled slightly left or right rather than straight back.

RAMIFICATION
Bonsai practitioners strive for good ramification—meaning they try to develop an intricate network of branches and twigs—to create the illusion of age. This sort of fine branching occurs naturally as trees grow slowly over many years, but bonsai artists work with young trees and must speed the process through pruning. Twiggy branches, along with the resulting short internodes (spaces between leaves) and small foliage, suggest age.

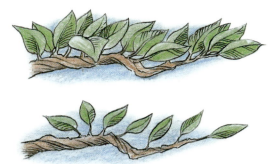

REVEALING FOLIAGE
Foliage that is too thick, as in the top example, obscures the branch structure. Proper pruning, as illustrated at bottom, produces a thinner stem bearing a sparser but more attractive foliage pad that shows off the woody structure. Excess leaves were cut off at their base and not across the leaf surface.

FOLIAGE

A bonsai's leaves should both reveal and complement the trunk and branch structure. A thick, bushy foliage mass obscures the structure and is indicative of a young tree. An open, airy canopy not only suggests age, but also promotes good air circulation to deter pests and keeps inner branchlets and leaves from being shaded and dying off. Very sparse coverage, however, gives the appearance of an unhealthy plant—and may indicate just such a condition.

Foliage should be in proportion to plant size. With the development of a good branching structure comes a reduction (modest in many cases) in leaf size. That's because the finer the shoot, the smaller the leaf. To a limited extent, leaf size can also be reduced through defoliation (see page 88). This is not a technique for beginners—and even in experienced hands, it should not be used as a permanent remedy for overlarge foliage.

For best results, choose small-leafed plants for training. Some of the best bonsai subjects are profiled in the chapter beginning on page 99.

ROOTS

A well-balanced root system, with a mix of thick, medium, and fine roots radiating in all directions, gives stability to a bonsai—an important consideration when growing a small tree in a small pot. Such a root system also indicates age and good health.

The appearance of roots, or even the suggestion of them, is important. You should be able to see clearly the point where a trunk starts to fan out into the root system. In many specimens, it is desirable to reveal the tops of large roots as they extend out from the trunk's base and down into the soil.

If a plant has an especially large and protruding root, face the root toward the back of the composition so it won't be a distraction. Or, at repotting time, cut the large root back (but not completely off) to weaken it; the tree will likely respond by strengthening the other roots or by sending out additional ones in other directions.

ASPECT: FRONT AND BACK

In nature, a tree can't be said to have a front or a back; it all depends on where the viewer stands. However, a bonsai is meant to be appreciated from one particular vantage point, so the issue of front or back is

The front of the cascade-style creeping juniper (Juniperus horizontalis), *seen in the top photograph, displays roots, foliage, and deadwood work on the trunk and branches to best advantage. The bottom photo shows the back, or less favored view, of the same plant.*

The mature root system of this Satsuki azalea (Rhododendron) *fans out in a radial pattern around the trunk.*

The shallow pot bearing a grove of Chinese elms (Ulmus parvifolia) *is a simple but elegant oval.*

important. The photos on page 18 illustrate this point.

When selecting a potential bonsai, and certainly when you begin training a plant, consider which side to face forward. The front should be the side with the greatest potential for displaying the plant's structure. It should be relatively open and show the largest flare of the trunk, the best radiating of roots, and the choicest view of the basic line of the tree and movement of the trunk.

Large roots that protrude forward, branches growing directly toward the viewer, and ungainly trunk curves that bulge out toward the front are considered undesirable.

Although the back of the plant will not be viewed directly, branches that grow toward the back are essential because they emphasize the third dimension. The branches should be well arranged—not simply a mass of twigs and leaves. Any awkwardly placed, ill-proportioned branches that might detract from the front view should be removed.

CONTAINER

A bonsai isn't a plant in just any pot. The container is part of the total artistic composition, as important as any element of the plant it contains. Pot selection always follows tree design, since the pot's function is to show the plant to best advantage.

Elaborately decorated pots were in vogue earlier in bonsai history, but they often stole the show. Now that the total composition is emphasized, a successful container is often one you hardly notice. Its shape may be rectangular, round, oval, square, or hexagonal. Some containers don't look like pots at all, such as those resembling a stone slab or crescent moon.

Some pots are fairly deep, especially ones designed to counterbalance cascading plants, while others seem impossibly shallow. You'll find both soft and intense colors. Glazed containers add sheen to the composition; unglazed ones are more unobtrusive. A pot may contain subtle ornamentation, such as bas-relief, or it may be perfectly plain. Of course, all good bonsai containers have drain holes.

Many choices are available in training pots and formal bonsai pots. (See pages 60 and 78 for examples of containers.) Those intended for training are usually a little larger and deeper to accommodate a larger root mass, though sometimes they just differ in quality. A bonsai typically spends several years in a less expensive training pot until it is ready for its ultimate container.

CHAPTER TWO

Understanding the Basics

THE ELEMENTS OF BONSAI CARE will be familiar to anyone who grows container plants—but because the growth of bonsai plants is so carefully controlled, each element takes on a special slant. ❧ This chapter contains basic information on day-to-day care. You'll learn how to choose the right outdoor site. You'll also find out what bonsai need in the way of soil mixes and watering and fertilizing regimes. Even more than ordinary potted plants, bonsai rely on meticulous pruning and pinching—techniques explained here. Pest and disease control is discussed, as is winter protection. ❧ You don't have to be an experienced gardener to maintain healthy bonsai—you can succeed if you cater to their needs. It also helps to have a rudimentary idea of how plants grow (see the illustration on page 23) to put some of the care into context.

The Right Site

Although you may want to display a plant indoors on special occasions, bonsai are not houseplants. Indoor temperature and humidity levels and inadequate light can quickly erode their health. Except when it's too cold for them, keep bonsai outdoors where they can thrive on fresh air and sunlight.

MODERATION

Avoid exposing bonsai to weather extremes. Locate plants away from high winds and pelting rain— or have alternative spots you can move them to during storms.

Provide as much sunlight as possible (especially in spring when plants are putting out new growth) without overheating or burning them. That can mean full sun where overcast, cool days are common. In sunnier, warmer areas, shelter plants from intense, summer-afternoon sun. A high-branching tree may provide enough shade, or you might need to build a simple structure with lath, latticework, bamboo screens,

or shade cloth to filter sunlight. Don't place plants where they might be overheated by sun reflecting off a wall.

INDIVIDUAL PLANT NEEDS

Give bonsai that require the most heat a warm location and shade lovers a more protected spot. Move them around as needed during the year, especially in climates where bonsai stay outdoors all year. Those getting summer shade can be shifted to better light in winter.

ELBOW ROOM

Don't crowd bonsai plants. Leave about 8 to 12 inches of space between the branch ends of adjacent plants so that each specimen can develop independently. Adequate space also promotes good plant health by allowing air to circulate and sunlight to penetrate to all parts of a bonsai.

ANIMALS

Take precautions to prevent animals from damaging bonsai. Keep plants raised on benches or tables where they won't be routinely exposed to house pets. To discourage a cat from jumping up, place wire mesh on the bench surface. If squirrels, raccoons, or deer visit your garden, locate bonsai where those animals have no access.

TOP: *This spacious "bonsai garden" includes sunny and shaded areas plus a table-height workbench.*

LEFT: *A lath overhang protects recently collected specimens from intense sunlight.*

How Plants Grow

A few facts about plant growth are helpful in understanding why gardeners—and bonsai practitioners—do what they do to maintain plants. The illustration below shows how a plant's main components (leaves, stems, and roots) work together as a unit and how air, water, sunlight, and soil come into play.

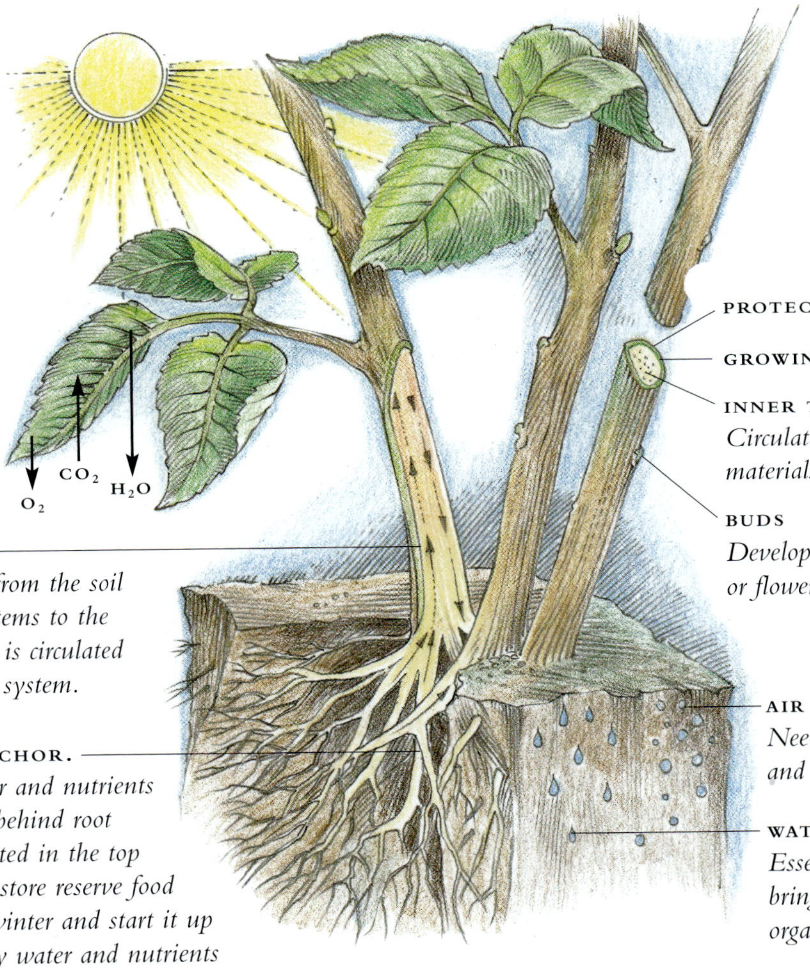

LEAVES MAKE FOOD. *Sunlight acts on green chlorophyll in leaves to convert raw materials absorbed from soil and air. This process is called photosynthesis.*

LEAVES "BREATHE." *Leaves draw in carbon dioxide from the air through pores and give off oxygen and water vapor. This is called transpiration.*

CO_2 H_2O O_2

STEMS ARE PLUMBING. *Nutrients and water taken from the soil by roots are drawn up the stems to the leaves. Food from the leaves is circulated through the plant by a duct system.*

ROOTS FEED, STORE, ANCHOR. *Roots feed by drawing water and nutrients from the soil through hairs behind root tips; root hairs are concentrated in the top part of the soil. Some roots store reserve food to carry the plant through winter and start it up in spring. Main roots convey water and nutrients in solution. They also hold the plant upright against wind and gravity. Because the roots of bonsai are pruned to keep the plant small and to fit into shallow pots, the plant is wired to the pot to anchor it.*

PROTECTIVE SKIN *(bark)*

GROWING LAYER *(cambium)*

INNER TISSUE *Circulates food and raw materials; stores food*

BUDS *Develop into leaves, stems, or flowers*

AIR *Needed by soil organisms and root tips*

WATER *Essential to plant; brings nutrients to soil organisms and roots*

SOIL SUSTAINS PLANT. *The plant relies on soil for support, water, and nutrients. How well soil sustains a plant depends on the soil's texture (compacted or open), water-holding capacity, readiness in releasing needed nutrients to the plant, and population of beneficial soil organisms.*

Potting Mixes

A bonsai needs soil that drains freely yet retains moisture. A mix made up mostly or entirely of drainage material—mineral particles like gravel or sand—allows free passage of water, but the water may drain too quickly. Adding organic matter like composted bark helps: it lodges between the mineral particles, absorbing water and holding it for use by plant roots. As organic matter decomposes, it supplies nutrients to the plant.

MAKING YOUR OWN MIX

You can buy potting mix sold specifically for bonsai, but blending your own mix is easy. Some bonsai hobbyists use equal parts of a packaged planting mix, river sand, and sifted fir or pine bark. Others mix equal parts of coarse gravel, high-fired baked clay, and sifted bark. These are only a couple of the myriad possibilities that provide plants with good drainage and organic matter.

What you choose will depend on what's available locally, how often you water, and the plants you're growing. Be sure not to use garden soil in your mix since it may contain soil pathogens. Also avoid ordinary potting mix, which is too fine. The basic particle sizes used in bonsai are $\frac{3}{16}$ to $\frac{1}{4}$ inch for standard mixes, and $\frac{1}{8}$ to $\frac{3}{16}$ inch for finer mixes.

DRAINAGE MATERIALS Popular choices include river sand, decomposed granite, lava, baked clay, perlite, and pumice. A material with sharp edges like decomposed

Among the many materials suitable for a bonsai mix are, left to right (top row) akadama soil (a type of pumice from Japan), black lava, pumice; (middle row) decomposed granite, red lava, large river sand; (bottom row) perlite, coarse landscape planting mix, fine fir bark (¼-inch pieces are often sold as "orchid bark"). All promote good drainage, and the landscape planting mix and fir bark also contribute organic matter.

Sift materials to get rid of pieces too small or too large to use in a potting mix. Here, a medium-mesh screen is used to filter perlite; the fine particles that fall through will be discarded. A large-mesh screen would be used to hold back over-size materials, such as big bark chunks.

granite retains moisture while a rounded material like sand doesn't. Thus, if you live in an arid climate or want to water less frequently, you would favor a material like decomposed granite over sand.

To make a grittier, faster-draining mix for certain plants, simply increase the proportion of drainage material or use a larger particle size. To tone down a material like perlite, which is bright white, top-dress with a darker drainage material, such as baked clay. The clay will also keep the lightweight perlite from floating during irrigation.

ORGANIC MATERIALS Composted bark is a favorite; pine bark is commonly used east of the Rockies and fir bark in the West. Although redwood bark is also widely available in the West, it's not recommended because it removes too much nitrogen that plant roots would otherwise absorb. Peat moss and oak leaf mold are often used in potting mixes for plants that require acidic conditions.

BASIC FORMULAS

If you're new to bonsai and want some standard mixes that will work well for most plants, follow these general ratios:

- 70 percent drainage material and 30 percent organic matter for evergreen plants.
- 60 percent drainage material and 40 percent organic matter for deciduous plants.

BEYOND THE BASIC

As you become more skilled in bonsai, experiment with potting mixes. For instance, depending on your climate, you might choose materials that warm up or stay cool. Or you might mix materials to achieve a desired color to complement plants or pots.

You might stratify a mix— layer several materials—to slow down drainage; water must saturate one layer before it can move down to the next one.

You'll also learn about specialty materials, such as kanuma, an acidic soil product from Japan that is popularly used in place of organic materials like peat moss or oak leaf mold for potting azaleas.

This pot contains 40 percent perlite, 35 percent fir bark, and—since false cypress (Chamaecyparis) appreciates organic matter—25 percent coarse planting mix. A top dressing of red and black lava harmonizes with the plant and the pot.

Watering

Bonsai have an even greater reliance on proper watering than ordinary container plants since they're planted in diminutive, often very shallow pots holding small amounts of potting mix.

HOW MUCH WATER?

All plants in containers need regular water—but deciduous ones with thin leaves like maple *(Acer)* usually need more water than average, and needle-leafed conifers like pine *(Pinus)* require less. With bonsai in larger pots, you may be able to stretch the intervals between watering, unless the soil is so infiltrated by roots that it dries out quickly. Younger plants need more frequent water than older ones. All bonsai demand more when newly planted or repotted than when their root systems are established.

The type of container can make a difference in water retention. Moisture will escape more quickly through an unglazed clay pot, for example, than through a glazed pot.

The hotter, drier, sunnier, or windier it is, the more rapidly plants transpire water through their leaves and the faster moisture evaporates from the soil. Thus, irrigate more often in a warm, dry-summer climate than in a cool, humid, foggy, or rainy one. Also water more often when the sun is intense than when there is cloud cover, and more often when the wind is blowing than when the air is still.

The amount of daylight influences watering needs, too. In

After watering the soil of a newly potted plant, moisten the foliage with a fine mist. Continue misting daily for several weeks until the plant has formed enough new roots to absorb all the water it needs.

equally hot weather, soil will remain moist longer in late summer and early fall than during the long days of early to mid-summer.

ONCE A DAY? TWICE? Depending on the conditions you encounter, you may have to water once a day or more often. Once-daily irrigation is best done in early morning; if watering again, do it in late afternoon. When the weather is cool or cloudy, you may need to water only every other day or so.

Check plants daily during the growing season. You don't want soil so dry that the plant wilts or so moist that the roots die from lack of air. Test the soil moisture with your fingertips. With small bonsai you can lift the pot; it will feel lighter when dried out and heavier when well watered.

If a bonsai is dry, water right away; if the soil is just slightly moist, water before it dries out completely. When the soil feels cool and damp, wait until it dries out more before watering.

WATERING METHODS

An automated drip system is sometimes used for large collections, but many bonsaiists prefer hand watering because it allows them to enjoy each plant and check it for pests and diseases at the same time.

Also, when hand watering you can water only those plants that need it and hold off on others. An automated system can't make that distinction.

Whichever method you choose, avoid artificially softened water or water treated with chemicals such as chlorine or sodium. If your house water is treated, hand-water with distilled water or collected rainwater. For drip irrigation, tap into your water pipe *before* your water softening or other treatment system.

HAND WATERING A long-spouted watering can with a fine-spray head allows you to water both the foliage and the soil by waving the can up and down over the plant. This keeps foliage free of dust, helps deter certain pests, and allows the plant to absorb some moisture through its leaves.

Rather than continually re-filling a watering can, you may prefer a garden hose with a nozzle that lets you flood the soil and gently spray the foliage. Get a nozzle that has a shut-off valve and isn't too big for your pots.

RIGHT: *Emitter line ringing a bonsai dispenses water slowly, in drips.*

BELOW RIGHT: *An electronic controller (popularly called a timer) automatically turns a watering system on and off. Be sure to alter the watering schedule as the weather and seasons change.*

Another option is to plunge the pot in a tub of water filled almost level with the pot rim. Let it stand in the tub for about 15 minutes, or until water has been drawn up the soil to the top. Routine watering by this method can cause potentially harmful salts to build up. To flush out impurities, sprinkle the soil at least every week or two. And don't forget to moisten the foliage periodically.

DRIP IRRIGATION Modern systems offer a choice of watering devices: individual emitters that drip water slowly (one per pot for small containers, two or more apiece for larger ones); emitter line, which has drip emitters installed inside at regular intervals; and spray nozzles that disperse water within a single pot.

You may also want to install special nozzles to mist foliage and reduce air temperature. Because the duration and timing of misting differ from that of watering, you will need separate circuits operated by different valves.

Automating your drip system will let you water even when you're not home, but it's no substitute for checking each bonsai. Have someone look in on your plants while you're away for any period of time.

Water Thoroughly

When watering by hand, keep applying water until it runs out the drain holes. Experienced bonsaiists will wait for the runoff to stop, then water again—and many will wait and water one more time. Be sure the soil mix is thoroughly moist and that water isn't just running down the insides of the pot—a sign that the plant needs repotting.

Fertilizing

Even though bonsai aren't supposed to grow big, they need nutrients to stay healthy and resist pests and diseases. These must be added since most drainage materials in potting mixes are sterile—and then replenished regularly since nutrients are leached by frequent watering.

DECIDING ON A FERTILIZER

Some dedicated bonsai enthusiasts make their own fertilizers from various organic ingredients, such as cottonseed meal, blood meal, and bonemeal. Others buy fertilizer pellets made especially for bonsai; see the photos below.

Most beginners will find it easy to apply a liquid fertilizer—either an organic one, such as fish emulsion, or one of the many commercially available inorganic fertilizers.

FEEDING REGULARLY

A plant needs the most fertilizer during its growing season. For tropical plants, that means feeding throughout the year since they grow all year. Feed other plants from early spring to early summer, and again in early fall.

Liquid fertilizer should be applied often. Give young specimens a product high in nitrogen every other week from early spring to early summer. More mature plants will thrive on the same regime, though they can get by with monthly applications. High-nitrogen fertilizers will produce leafy growth at the expense of flowers or fruit, so give bonsai

Fertilizer pellets contain soluble nutrients that leach into the soil with each watering. Start with one pellet in each corner of a small rectangular pot like the one shown here; you'd use more in the larger oval pot. Apply the pellets in early spring, adding the same number each month until spring is over—by then, 4 will have grown to 12. Then discard the pellets. Repeat in early fall; stop after the first month in cold-winter areas but add more pellets during fall in mild climates.

Reading Labels

Fertilizer labels list the percentages of major nutrients as a series of three numbers—such as 10–5–5, 15–0–0, or 0–10–10. Nitrogen is indicated by the first number, phosphorus (as phosphoric acid) by the second, and potassium (as potash) by the third.

grown for those features a more balanced fertilizer.

Hold off feeding in summer (except in cool climates), then apply a fertilizer high in phosphorus and potassium and with little or no nitrogen in early fall. If desired, continue feeding where winters are mild.

Remember, don't feed a sick tree or one that's under stress—for example, after it has been overwatered, underwatered, or recently repotted.

EASY DOES IT

Be cautious when using liquid fertilizer. It's better to overdilute than underdilute. The safest approach is to use twice the amount of water recommended on the product label, creating a half-strength solution to avoid any possibility of damaging roots. Whatever you use in spring, use about half as much in fall.

Feed in early morning after watering. Using a watering can with a fine-spray head, apply the solution to the soil until the excess liquid flows out the pot's drain hole.

Pests and Diseases

Bonsai are subject to the same pests and diseases as their full-size garden counterparts. But because the plants are small and portable, controlling these problems is often easier.

IDENTIFYING PROBLEMS

Considering the range of plants used in bonsai and the many growing regions, it's difficult to generalize about pests and diseases. Among the most widespread pests, however, are aphids (particularly in spring), spider mites (in summer), scale insects, and mealybugs. Powdery mildew is a common disease.

Refer to a comprehensive garden book for help identifying a problem and control measures. Or take the plant to a local nursery or fellow bonsai practitioners to find out what's wrong.

FIGHTING PESTS

Try the easiest method first. Remove larger pests by hand. Hose off smaller ones, such as aphids and mites, with a jet of water; repeat several times at 2- or 3-day intervals.

If you choose a spray other than water, try the one least dangerous to organisms other than the target pest. A solution of insecticidal soap or liquid dishwashing detergent (2 tablespoons in 1 gallon of water) will kill soft-bodied insects and the larvae of scale insects. Both substances kill by contact, so a thorough application is necessary; rinse off the plant with water about an

hour after spraying. Light horticultural oils, called summer oils, operate in the same manner.

If you opt for a stronger pesticide, you have a choice of botanical insecticides (made from plants) or synthetics. Read labels to determine what the product kills beyond your intended target, then use the one that causes the least collateral damage. Also check the product's residual life.

No matter what type of spray you use, be sure the bonsai is well watered before you apply it. Move the plant to a shaded area, and spray during a cool time of day.

FIGHTING DISEASES

Disease controls are continually changing. New products come on the market as others are withdrawn. Consult a reputable nursery or your county agricultural agent to learn about the most effective control currently available for your problem.

Removing spent flowers and cleaning up debris will not only neaten this camellia, but it will also help prevent a disease, camellia petal blight.

Avoiding Problems

Here are some simple preventive measures:
- Use pots that have one or more good-size drain holes. Standing water can lead to root rot.
- Before reusing a pot, clean it to get rid of any damaging organisms that may be present. Remove any old soil with hot water and a brush. Then swab the inside of the container with a 10 percent solution of chlorine bleach and rinse well.
- Prune and pinch as needed to keep the interior of plants open to sunlight and for good air circulation.
- Clean up plant debris promptly.
- Inspect bonsai frequently and take care of any problems right away.

Pruning and Pinching

Gardeners are familiar with manipulating plant growth by pruning and pinching, techniques also used in training bonsai. Pruning is used on hard, woody stems and pinching on soft growth.

PRUNING

Minor pruning consists of snipping out unnecessary small branches or twigs to open up the plant. It can be an annual event, or an ongoing activity if you have plants that regularly produce dense growth.

Major pruning involves removing entire branches to effect a more dramatic change. You'll do this when converting nursery stock or plants collected from the wild into bonsai specimens. This initial pruning establishes a plant's basic shape by removing non-essential and unattractive branches. It is also the time to eliminate overly large branches, since coarse growth only produces more coarse growth.

You may need to make more major cuts over the years as you refine your plant and as small branches develop that can be used to replace larger ones.

With major pruning there's no turning back. Once a branch is removed, it's gone for good. So study a plant carefully, analyzing its potential shape, before you make any major alterations.

WHEN TO PRUNE Minor pruning whenever it's needed won't hurt a plant, but be more careful about major pruning. For most plants, major cuts are best made toward the end of a plant's dormancy—the period when it is not actively growing.

It's easy to see when a deciduous plant is dormant—it is leafless then. Although evergreen plants keep their leaves, they typically slow down growth to a level approaching dormancy during the coldest time of year (species native to mild or tropical regions may do so at other times).

Close, year-round observation of your plants is your best guide to their periods of dormancy. Also consult the individual plant listings in the chapter beginning on page 99 for specific information about when to prune.

FROM COARSE TO FINE
Careful pruning and pinching will allow you to create graceful transitions from coarse to fine growth—from large trunk to large branches to smaller branches to branchlets and finally to twigs.

To prevent or minimize bark scarring from major pruning, use sharp pruning tools to make clean cuts.

ABOVE TOP: *Remove unwanted growth such as suckers and water sprouts. Suckers are upright shoots arising from the roots or underground stem of a woody plant; water sprouts are vigorous, upright, usually weakly attached shoots growing on a branch or along the trunk. If you get to them soon enough, you can pinch or rub them off.*

ABOVE BOTTOM: *When removing branches, make closer cuts than you would in general gardening, since every protuberance is more noticeable on bonsai. Concave cutters and knob cutters, which leave a slightly cupped indentation, make the closest cuts. The indentation becomes virtually flat after bark has grown to cover the cut.*

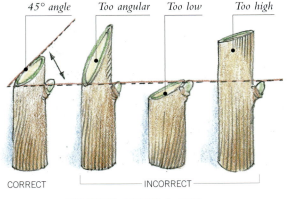

TYPES OF CUTS

Shown here are three types of cuts: pinching removes the terminal growth; heading removes part of the shoot, and thinning eliminates the entire shoot.

CUTTING ABOVE A BUD

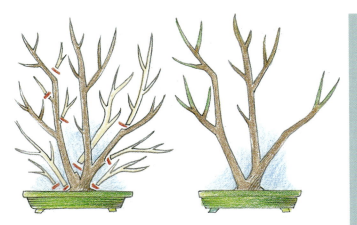

THINNING

Thinning removes an entire stem or branch back to its point of origin or to a junction with another branch. These cuts open up a plant and cause the least amount of regrowth.

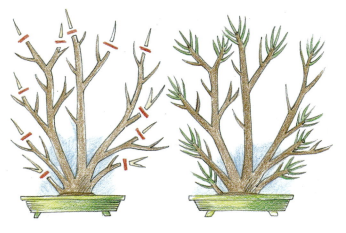

HEADING

Heading removes part of a stem or branch back to a bud, twig, or branchlet. Each cut produces a cluster of shoots where you've cut or from buds below it.

Wound Callusing

Just as your own skin forms a protective scab when cut, a plant responds to a wound by callusing over—forming a thickened tissue that seals off the wound. As you would expect, smaller wounds seal more quickly than bigger ones. Here are ways to encourage wound callusing on your bonsai:

- Make clean cuts with well-sharpened pruning tools.
- Cover the wound with one of the protective, puttylike compounds (some sold as "cut paste") available through bonsai suppliers. As the callus forms, it pushes off the coating.
- Don't make too many cuts at one time; or, if you've made a large cut, put any more pruning on hold until the main wound calluses.
- Preserve any growth that sprouts on a large wound for a year before pruning it off.
- Keep bonsai well watered and fertilized; healthy trees will callus over wounds more quickly.

The tall shoot above the large pruning cut on this European beech (Fagus sylvatica) has been allowed to grow unimpeded, helping the large pruning wound callus over. Once the tree has recovered, the escaped leader will be cut back.

LEFT: *Thumb and forefinger are the primary pinching tools. Other pinching tools include tweezers for pinching out the smallest, softest growth, and cuticle scissors or small bonsai trimmers for making clean cuts in small, tight spaces.*

RIGHT: *This strong shoot will be pinched back to encourage a smaller one to grow in its place.*

PINCHING

Nipping off the soft growing tip of a shoot redirects growth into buds just below the pinch, resulting in two or more new shoots branching off the original one. Thus, pinching is vital in controlling the direction of new growth once you've roughed out a bonsai style. If you start with a small, young plant, you'll probably be able to do a great deal of the shaping you want just by pinching.

Remove overlong growth—especially common on deciduous trees—as soon as you see it. Pinch off shoot tips to create branching where you want it. Also pinch off much of the new growth that would grow toward the plant's interior, cluttering the plant's structure. Rub off any unwanted growth sprouting from a branch or trunk.

Generally, you can pinch off leafy new growth as needed anytime during the growing season. Depending on the plant and the time of year, new growth may appear beneath the pinch within several weeks or the next growing season.

FLOWERS By all means, let flowers bloom the first year to see what you have. For the next few years, however, pinch off the flower buds so that the plant's energy will go into developing the trunk and branches. After that, pinch off flower buds every other year or so for best bloom production over the long term.

Flowers and Fruit

Pruning won't reduce the size of flowers or fruit, unless you prune so heavily that you also weaken the plant. Camellias, for example, will display full-size blossoms—a reason to choose a small-flowered variety. To avoid too large a disproportion between fruit and plant, bonsaiists usually select plants with relatively small fruit, such as cotoneaster, kumquat (*Fortunella*), or crabapple (*Malus*), shown below.

PINCHING
The terminal bud at the tip of a shoot causes that shoot to grow in length. Pinching off the tip stops that growth and stimulates branching.

Winter Protection

Plants in containers are more subject to cold damage than the same plants growing in the ground, because pots just don't hold enough soil to insulate plant roots. That's why even frost-tolerant plants grown as bonsai need shelter when the weather turns wintry.

Heat cables keep these small, broad-leafed evergreen bonsai warmer than they would be on the bark mulch or tabletop.

COLD DAMAGE

Where winters are frost free or relatively mild (above 20°F/–7°C), bonsai can be left outdoors without any special protection. But bonsai need safeguarding in colder climates.

Some plants, especially broad-leafed evergreens, may die if their roots are exposed to freezing soil temperatures. Frozen soil can be a hazard to any plant that bears leaves in winter: freezing locks up soil moisture, making it impossible for leaves to replace moisture they lose through transpiration.

KEEPING BONSAI OUTDOORS

Where winter lows are in the range of 10°F/–12°C to 20°F/ –7°C, you can keep bonsai outdoors. But surround pots of broad-leafed evergreen bonsai with a mulch of tree bark, pine needles, leaves, sawdust, or other lightweight material to insulate the soil and minimize freezing. (Avoid using straw since it attracts mice.) Plants beneath an over-hang, such as house eaves or tree foliage, will remain warmer than plants exposed to open sky.

BRINGING BONSAI INDOORS

Winter temperatures that normally fall below 10°F/–12°C can damage or kill exposed bonsai. Broad-leafed evergreens are the first victims; needle-leafed evergreens and deciduous plants are

Watering in Winter

During freezing weather, water your bonsai (if they need it) in the morning. This allows excess water to drain out before the temperature drops. Water-soaked soil expands as it freezes, which can cause containers to crack.

more cold-tolerant, but they are still vulnerable.

The best place to overwinter bonsai is an unheated structure. A greenhouse is ideal; the plants receive good light, are somewhat protected from the cold, and with a door ajar or vents open slightly get plenty of air. A cold frame works much like a low greenhouse; a hinged translucent top lets in light and can be opened for ventilation. It is most effective placed against a south-facing house wall and nestled into the ground over a thick bed of gravel. A garage or shed—ideally with a window—can also be used.

A table overhead and bark mulch surrounding the pots help protect these bonsai from winter cold.

CHAPTER THREE

Getting Started

YOU MAY BE READY *to dive headlong into bonsai, but take it slowly. Get just the tools and supplies you'll need as a beginner. You can always obtain additional equipment as you learn more about bonsai and figure out which items will be most useful.* ❧ *The go-slow approach also applies to bonsai techniques. Don't try to do too much to a plant all at once. Cutting off most of the root ball and severely pruning back the top may be fine for experts, but beginners must first learn to keep bonsai plants alive and well before stressing them.* ❧ *In this chapter, you'll find out how to choose plants and which tools are essential. There is also detailed information on wiring, training plants according to each of the five basic styles in the classic Japanese model, and repotting. Plus you'll find an introduction to one of the up-and-coming areas of specialization, tropical bonsai.*

Choosing Plants

As you gain experience in bonsai, you may want to start your own specimens from seeds, cuttings, or other propagation methods, but beginners will find it easier and faster to start with nursery plants.

SUITABLE STOCK

Many nurseries carry small specimens labeled "bonsai plants" in 2- to 4-inch pots; some will have just a single stem and a tuft of foliage, while others may show the beginnings of a branch structure.

But don't restrict yourself to that selection. Plants suitable for bonsai come in all sizes, whether or not they're tagged as such. Look among 1- to 5-gallon container stock for possible candidates; the checklist at right will help you narrow your choices.

Also consult the encyclopedia beginning on page 99 for plants with a proven track record. Remember, while almost any tree or shrub in a nursery could conceivably be trained as a bonsai, not all will turn into good bonsai even given your best efforts. For example, some species may grow too fast or have very large leaves.

A FUTURE BONSAI?

Once you've made a few initial selections, examine each for training potential. Look at the plant's basic structure to see if it suggests a particular style of training, keeping in mind that you'll probably have to remove

Checklist

Look for these features in a nursery plant:

- Healthy appearance, not too lanky or sparse.
- Trunk noticeably wider at the bottom, tapering to a narrow top; not too tall.
- Good root system but not root-bound; pull the plant out of the nursery pot to make sure it does not have circling or strangling roots.
- Small leaves and twiggy branches—they are better suited to bonsai than big leaves and coarse branches. Pass up plants with compound leaves (large leaves divided into small leaflets) until you have more experience.
- Climate suitability (nurseries often stock plants from other regions that gardeners may want but will struggle locally).

some branches and bend parts of the plant to accentuate a form. Rotate the plant to see if one side would make a good front (see "Aspect" on page 18).

As a beginner, you may want to stick with plants for which you have a reasonably clear plan in mind. With experience, you may decide on plants that appeal to you, even if you're not sure how you'll train them.

This nursery display shows assorted plants suitable for bonsai training.

Tools

*As a beginner, you can get by nicely with just a few basic tools.
You won't know the full range of implements you'll really need—
or want—until you've worked at bonsai for a while.*

KEEP IT SIMPLE

Start with just the few primary tools you'll need to get through the first year or so. You can add to your collection as you learn new techniques requiring specialized tools. And, as you progress, you can always replace any inexpensive starter tools with better-quality items.

Some of the implements you'll use are designed especially for bonsai, such as concave cutters for making very close pruning cuts. Other tools are familiar items originally intended for other purposes—for instance, chopsticks for teasing apart roots and for tamping soil mix into air pockets. An inexpensive plastic turntable sold with kitchen utensils is handy for rotating plants, even if it doesn't have a stop to hold the plant in place.

You may have some general gardening tools that you can use for bonsai, such as pruning shears and a small handsaw.

NEAT AND CLEAN

Tools last longer and work better when properly maintained. After using your tools, clean them with soapy water or rubbing alcohol and dry them before storing. Keep metal tools rust-free by wiping them with an oily rag. Sharpen cutting blades regularly with a whetstone.

Keeping your tools in a caddy or pouch will protect them and lessen the chance of misplacing or losing any items.

A beginner needs only the few basic tools shown here: an inexpensive turntable (A), concave cutters (B), pruning shears (C), side-cutting pliers (D), pointy-tipped chopsticks (E), coils of aluminum wire with a coppery finish (F), wound sealant (G), pruning scissors (H), and a handsaw (I). You could hold off on getting concave cutters—the costliest item here—if you prefer to wait awhile to invest in good tools.

Wiring

At this stage, you'll do basic wiring on the trunk and branches to force them into the positions you want. Take care because branches may break. Try practicing on limber branches of a garden tree or shrub.

WHEN TO WIRE

The best time to work on deciduous trees is the late dormant season when the trees are leafless and you can see clearly what you're doing. Evergreens should also be wired then so that the wires are in place before spring growth begins.

Avoid wiring a plant while it's putting on new growth that could be damaged. Wait to wire soft, new growth until it has firmed up the following year.

COPPER OR ALUMINUM?

Although copper is the traditional wire of bonsai, aluminum wire with a coppery finish is growing in popularity. Both are sold through nurseries, garden centers, hardware stores, and bonsai supply companies.

Aluminum wire is easier for beginners to use since it is always flexible and can be removed and rewrapped to correct mistakes. But it isn't as strong as copper, so you must use more of it. The coppery finish on the aluminum also fades to silver within months.

Along with being stronger, copper wire acquires the patina of oxidation as it ages. But it must be treated by annealing before it can be used, and it is much less flexible than aluminum afterward.

Previously, bonsaiists had to treat copper wire themselves, but annealed wire is now widely sold. If you want to anneal copper yourself, make a fire of tightly wrapped newspapers and place the coil of wire in the fire. After the flames have turned blue, remove the wire and let it cool. Don't unwind or bend the treated wire until you are ready to use it.

CHOOSING A SIZE

The wire size you need depends on the thickness of the trunk or branch: choose heavier wire for trunks and thicker branches, and thinner wire for slender, pliable

Dealing with Breaks

Even when you're careful, you may bend a branch to its breaking point while wiring. If the break is simply a fracture and the broken part is still partially attached, you have a chance to save the branch.

Unwrap the wire from the branch. Ease the broken part into place, fitting the broken ends together. Wrap the break with garden tape or raffia and tie it securely but not too tightly. Within several months, the fractured tissue may knit together. If it does, don't try to wire or bend it—the branch will break again.

If the break is complete or the ends fail to knit together, you can cut the broken branch back to a side branch or to its point of origin. Or you might consider making the branch into *jin* (see page 70).

branches. Use the lightest possible wire that will hold a bend in place. Flex the trunk or branch and choose a wire that is about as flexible.

The thickness of copper wire is expressed as a gauge. The lower the gauge, the thicker the wire. For example, #8 wire is heavy and should be used only

Coils of annealed and oxidized copper wire in a variety of gauges are ready for use.

Wire holds a shaped trunk and branches in the desired positions.

for a trunk or large branches, while #16 is light and suitable for very thin branches.

Aluminum wire is measured in millimeters. The lower the number, the thinner the wire. For instance, #1 is extremely fine and #5 thick. Because aluminum wire is so flexible, you must use a thicker size or more strands to hold bends than you would with copper wire, especially when wiring springy branches like those of many conifers.

GETTING READY TO WIRE

A trunk or branch should be warm prior to bending. Massaging it in one direction to warm it is better than bending it back and forth, which may crack the cambium (the green layer of growth cells under the bark) on both sides of the limb.

If a limb bends as far as you want, there shouldn't be any difficulty wiring it into that position. Even if you encounter resistance, you should still be able to wire it if you choose the right thickness of wire and apply it properly.

To avoid bruising or scarring thin-barked plants like azaleas *(Rhododendron)* and maples *(Acer),* cover the wire with self-adhesive florist's tape before wrapping it around a limb. Where wire will apply too much pressure to a bend, wrap the branch with raffia first to pad it.

HOW TO WIRE

To wire a bonsai, begin below the lowest point to be trained and work upward. For each section that's to be wired, you'll need a piece of wire about 1½ times as long as that section. Be sure to use the appropriate size wire for the trunk or branch.

Secure the wire by wrapping it around the trunk below a branch, if there is one, or jamming about 2 inches of wire into the soil at the back of the plant, taking care not to damage the roots.

Wrap the wire in a spiral at about a 45-degree angle, maintaining a uniform distance between coils. Wrap clockwise if

WIRING A BEND
Be sure wire coils on the outside of a limb at each point where you will exert pressure and bend it (see Xs on illustration). The wire will also hold the bends in place. On a cascading trunk, such as the one illustrated here, you may have multiple points that will be bent.

you intend to bend the limb clockwise, and counterclockwise for a bend in that direction. (If you wrap one way and bend the other, the wire will come loose.) Make the wrap snug but not too taut, as the wire will tighten when you make the bend.

When wiring a branch, face the branch toward you; use one hand to guide the wire around the branch and the other to hold the coils tightly in place. As you progress, start bending the branch the way you want it to go.

Once the branch is completely wired, you can make the final bend. Hold the limb firmly and place both thumbs at the place you want to bend it. Gradually bend the branch into position by repeatedly pushing in one direction. Bending in a single session is better than doing it over time, though sometimes you won't be able to bend the branch enough in one session.

Spiral scars result when wire remains in place more than one growing season while branch diameter increases.

REMOVING THE WIRE

To give wired limbs a chance to grow into their new positions, leave the wiring in place for a full growing season, but check often for girdling.

In early fall, remove the wires to avoid any constriction during the next growth phase. Snip off stiff copper wire, to avoid inflicting damage by uncoiling. Thick aluminum wire can also be cut off, but smaller sizes may be unwrapped, starting from the outermost ends.

Wired branches that still need more coaxing to achieve the desired positions can be rewired at the appropriate time for another season of training. When you rewire a branch, vary the position from that of the previous year if the wire left even the slightest marks.

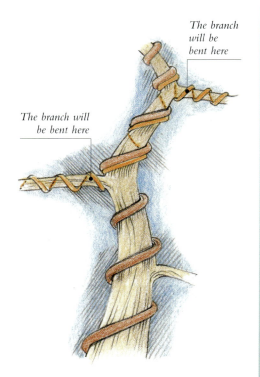

The branch will be bent here

The branch will be bent here

WIRING BRANCH TO BRANCH

To wire two nearby branches use a single piece of wire. Wrap it around the trunk at least once, to anchor the branches so they won't pull on each other, then wire each branch.

Don't overlap any trunk wire. If you wired the trunk, you should have placed the wire consistently either just above or just below each branch. When the trunk wire is positioned above the branch crotch, as shown here, wrap the branch wire just below the trunk wire. If you wired below the branch crotch, wrap the branch wire just above the trunk wire.

Bending a Stiff Branch

A branch too difficult to bend by wiring can often be given a simple downward bend by securing it with wire to an anchor, usually either the trunk or the pot. You can use thinner wire to do this than you would for wiring a branch.

Massage the branch where you want to bend it, and push firmly with your thumbs in one direction; attach the wire using one of the methods described below. If you can't bend the branch far enough, try putting a turnbuckle on the wire. Turn it gradually over time to bring the branch into the desired position.

Wire looped through the drain holes and encircling the branch holds the limb firmly in place. The turnbuckle is used to bend the branch further.

TYING TO THE TRUNK *Encircle the branch with a padded wire loop, bend the branch down, and attach the wire to the trunk. Also place padding between the wire and the trunk.*

TYING TO THE POT *The neatest arrangement is a wire running through the drain holes, then up through the soil and around the branch in a padded loop, as shown in the photo above.*

A less elegant method is to loop a strand of wire under the pot and up over the soil, tie the ends together snugly, then loop a separate wire around the branch and attach it to the pot wire.

Five Basic Styles

The easiest styles for beginners are the basic Japanese ones pictured on the following pages. Styles requiring more expertise are described in the subsequent chapters.

Your plant might lend itself to a slanting style, as this cotoneaster does.

STEP BY STEP

The temptation to bare-root a starter plant at the same time you style the top—so that you can fit it into a bonsai pot for an "instant bonsai"—may be powerful. But resist subjecting a plant to that much stress until you've gained more experience. By training a plant slowly, you'll increase your chances of success at every step.

If you've dug your specimen from the garden, transfer it to an ordinary clay pot before you style the top.

The first step with a nursery plant is to take it out of its pot and examine the root system. If it's in good shape, put the plant back in its original container and leave it there for the first year or so, until it needs repotting (see pages 54–55).

In some cases, you may have to unwrap circling roots or score the outside of a dense root ball before returning it to its pot. If you lose some of the nursery soil in the process, fill in with coarse planting mix.

MAKING CUTS

Since the root system is basically intact, you can work the top right away. Eliminate superfluous growth as you start developing the style you're following. See pages 30–32 for information on pruning and pinching.

Don't make too many major cuts. If in doubt about which branches to remove, take off large branches from the top and small branches from the bottom. If you can't decide between two branches, leave both and see which develops better. Retain some extra branches to nourish the plant; you can prune off these at a later date.

WIRING

You will use wire to hold in place the various bends you make in the trunk and branches. Aluminum wire is more flexible than copper and easier for beginners to manipulate. For more information about wiring, see pages 38–40.

Formal Upright

A majestic tree standing alone in a field or lawn epitomizes this style. The chief characteristic is a straight trunk that tapers gradually as it rises. The trunk base splays outward just enough to indicate that radiating roots give good support.

The branches are longer and thicker at the bottom, becoming shorter and more closely spaced as they approach the top, giving the tree an overall cone shape. Branches on opposite sides of the trunk are not at the same level, and no branch is directly above another one.

PLANTS Trees that naturally grow straight and tall are good candidates. These include dwarf Alberta spruce *(Picea glauca albertiana 'Conica')*, pictured here, as well as fir *(Abies)*, beech *(Fagus)*, juniper *(Juniperus)*, larch *(Larix)*, sweet gum *(Liquidambar)*, pine *(Pinus)*, coast redwood *(Sequoia sempervirens)*, and bald cypress *(Taxodium distichum)*.

1 A healthy, densely foliaged dwarf Alberta spruce is ready for styling.

2 Remove the plant from its pot and clear the top soil with chopsticks to expose the root crown and trunk flare. This deters crown rot and helps you find the front of the plant.

3 After choosing the front (in this case, the side with the best view of the surface roots), snip off any weak roots.

4 If the plant is too tall, choose a vertical branch as the new leader, then prune off the top of the plant. Make the cut behind the leader to hide the pruning wound. In time the wound will callus over.

5 Thin the plant by pruning off some branches; leave others for later removal. Here, a large branch near the top is eliminated—it would have caused the upper trunk to thicken.

6 If a new leader was chosen, wire the trunk to position the top in line with the lower trunk. Anchor the wire by jamming the end into the soil. Choose wire thick enough to hold the trunk upright.

7 Wire the main branches. Use slightly thicker wire on the bigger branches than on the smaller ones.

8 Position the branches by exerting thumb pressure on the wire. Slope the branches downward to suggest age.

9 Since the root ball is intact, there's no need to add soil mix when replacing the plant in its pot.

Informal Upright

This style—the easiest for novices—is a relaxed version of the formal upright. The trunk may display a slight curve, a bit of a slant, or both; many good specimens have trunks shaped like an elongated "S." The top should be in a direct line over the base, or close to it.

The general branch arrangement described for the formal upright style applies here. Branching from the outside of the trunk's curve rather than from the inside is preferred. Avoid a front-facing bulge between the soil and first branch (called a "pigeon breast").

PLANTS Along with deodar cedar *(Cedrus deodara)*, pictured here, choices include false cypress *(Chamaecyparis)*, winter hazel *(Corylopsis)*, witch hazel *(Hamamelis)*, crabapple *(Malus)*, pine *(Pinus)*, Chinese quince *(Pseudocydonia sinensis)*, oak *(Quercus)*, azalea *(Rhododendron)*, and yew *(Taxus)*.

1 A deodar cedar is ready to be styled. Since the trunk is fairly straight, it will have to be bent to become an informal upright.

2 Unpot the plant and use chopsticks to clear the crown area of soil, moss, and small roots wrapping around the trunk. Cut any large circling roots like the ones shown here. Replace the plant in its pot.

3 Snip off some unneeded small branches to clear a path for wiring the trunk. On a sparsely branched specimen like this, you won't need to remove much growth.

4 Choose wire thick enough to hold the bend you will be making in the trunk. Anchor the wire in the soil; wire the trunk. If the tree is too tall and you intend to cut back the trunk, wire only to that point.

5 Use thumb pressure to shape the trunk. Exaggerate the first bend since it will spring back somewhat when you make the next bend.

6 Keep bending until you achieve the desired shape, keeping in mind that the top should end up roughly over the base. The branches will change positions when the trunk is bent; decide which ones to keep.

7 Carefully wire the branches that will be retained, threading in and out of the needles to avoid crushing them.

8 If the specimen is too tall, cut back the top. Snip off some of the unwired branches; others may be left to nourish the plant.

9 Bend the wired branches into place.

10 Let the tree develop before doing any more pruning. Plan on shortening some branches in the future as side growth forms.

Slanting

The lean can be a subtle one in response to the sun, or a more dramatic one due to eroding soil. In either case, the tree top should fall in a line well clear of the base. If one side of the tree has larger roots, that side should be opposite the slant—otherwise, there would be no reason for the tree to stand.

The branches should be arranged in horizontal layers that are parallel to the ground or bend slightly downward. The concentration of weight should be on the side away from the slant, to counterbalance the lean—though the longest branches can reach in the direction of the slant.

PLANTS *Juniperus procumbens* 'Nana', shown here, is a good candidate, as are Japanese maple *(Acer palmatum)*, cedar *(Cedrus)*, Chinese hackberry *(Celtis sinensis)*, cotoneaster, larch *(Larix)*, spruce *(Picea)*, pine *(Pinus)*, and yew *(Taxus)*.

1 Because junipers are so tough, beginners can remove three-quarters or so of the branches from a dense specimen like this without harming the plant.

2 Take the plant out of its container and prune off bottom branches that are obscuring the crown. Here, a branch that sprouted at the base to form an extra trunk is removed. Clear the crown area with chopsticks. Return the plant to its container.

3 Decide on the front of the plant. This plant has been rotated so that a crimp in the trunk faces toward the back. Snip off unnecessary branches.

4 Wire the trunk. In this case, only the upper trunk will be wired since the lower trunk has a curve suitable for the slanting style. Anchor the wire under a branch at midtrunk and work upward.

5 Wire the branches that you intend to keep.

6 Grasp the trunk firmly and exert thumb pressure to bend it.

7 Bend the wired branches into position.

8 Cut off the superfluous growth at the top. If necessary, first twist the trunk so that the pruning cut will be hidden when the plant faces front.

9 Do any necessary touch-up work. Here, some additional small branches are wired and others cut off.

10 The styled tree has an obvious slant.

Semicascade

This style represents trees that grow on steep slopes or overhang water. The trunk starts to ascend, then seemingly succumbs to gravity—but less dramatically than a full cascade (see pages 50–51).

In a semicascade the descending trunk is nearly horizontal or pendent; the branches and trunk apex fall somewhere between the soil line and the midway point of the container.

1 A very dense juniper is ready for styling. Have handy a heavy clay pot big enough to hold the plastic nursery pot and keep the plant from tipping over while you're working on it.

2 If the root ball is in good shape like this one, it can be left alone. Remove some lower branches for a better view of the root crown.

3 Prune off much of the growth along the trunk so you can see its shape and to make wiring easier. A dogleg—an abrupt bend—in the trunk is now visible, one of the reasons this particular specimen was chosen for a semicascade.

PLANTS *Juniperus procumbens* 'Nana', shown here, as well as natal plum *(Carissa macrocarpa)*, cedar *(Cedrus)*, cotoneaster, cypress *(Cupressus)*, firethorn *(Pyracantha)*, and azalea *(Rhododendron)*, are among the plants lending themselves to this style.

4 Use wire thick enough to weigh down the trunk and hold it in place. Anchor the wire in the soil. Be sure to coil wire on top of the dogleg since strong bending pressure will be exerted there.

5 Bend the trunk into the desired position. Cut a notch in the plastic pot to get the trunk lower than the pot rim.

6 As you bend the trunk, branches will change position. Here, a prominent now-upright shoot is pruned off.

7 Decide which branches to keep; wire and reposition them as desired. Thin out some excess growth. The plant is now in the clay pot to keep it steady.

8 Cut off the apex if it is too long and bushy, as is the case here. Growth should be finer and finer toward the end, and the trunk line more visible.

9 If you think the plant needs it, tweak it by bending some wired branches and shortening others. Here, a few shoots near the dogleg are being wired; they will be bent to soften the sharp angle of the bend and hide the pruning wound.

10 This semicascade seems to flow horizontally before descending a bit.

Cascade

Only a few inches of trunk grow upward before a cascade starts to arch over the edge of a container and flow abruptly downward. The trunk apex and branches extend below the bottom of the pot.

This style is patterned after "mountain goat" trees, which cling to cliff faces and are forced downward by landslides, snowslides, and their tenuous grasp on scant soil. But, while the trunk grows down, the branch ends turn up, giving the appearance of a plant trying to right itself.

3 Cut off any excess roots. Here, a second set of roots that started along the trunk is removed.

4 Prune off unneeded growth at the top of the plant.

5 Remove yellowed foliage in areas that were shaded inside the plant.

6 Start wiring the trunk near where the top was pruned off; place the coil on top of the spot where downward pressure will be applied. (Don't wire the lower section of trunk since it won't be bent.)

7 After wiring along the apex, wire small branches that you intend to keep.

8 Bend all along the length of the trunk to shape the cascade downward.

9 If there's a shoot competing with the cascade, shorten or remove it. Here, the plant has been rotated and a shoot cut off.

10 With the plant facing front again, do any refinement shaping by pinching with your fingers.

PLANTS Many plants can be encouraged to cascade, such as *Juniperus procumbens* 'Nana', shown here. Others include sasanqua *(Camellia sasanqua),* cedar *(Cedrus),* some species of cotoneaster, Japanese black pine *(Pinus thunbergii),* and firethorn *(Pyracantha).*

1 This very dense juniper has a growth habit lending itself to cascade styling. About three-quarters of the growth will be removed.

2 Prune off some lower branches so you can see the top of the root ball better. Tease the root crown with chopsticks.

Tropical Bonsai

This increasingly popular area of specialization involves training true tropical species as well as subtropical ones and plants that are adapted to indoor growing.

NOT JUST FOR THE TROPICS

In warm-weather regions of the world, many hobbyists have turned to tender plants growing locally for bonsai specimens, rather than the maples, pines, and other plants native to temperate climates traditionally used in Japanese bonsai.

The experiment has been so successful that tropical bonsai as a distinct form of the art has taken off in Southeast Asia, India, South America, Mexico, and Puerto Rico, as well as Hawaii, southern Florida, and along the Gulf Coast into Corpus Christi, Texas.

This form of bonsai has also found enthusiasts in cold-winter areas. Here, the definition of tropical bonsai is stretched to include just about any

temperate-area plant that takes well to indoor culture, such as boxwood *(Buxus)*.

Even in warm areas, some temperate plants are often included with tender ones in a bonsai collection. But choose plants suited to your climate—for example, species that need winter chilling won't succeed in areas like southern Florida.

TROPICAL STYLES

Many hobbyists style plants naturally, recalling their appearance in the wild. Some train certain plants naturally and other plants according to the classic Japanese model—or other models. How to style a particular plant is usually a matter of personal preference, or perhaps local practice.

Ficus neriifolia

WINTER CARE

In the warmest regions, plants can stay outdoors in winter, although it's prudent to protect the most tender ones if a cold spell is expected. Some hobbyists move them to a green-house or other protected area when temperatures are expected to fall below 40°F/4°C.

In wintry climates, bring plants indoors for the cold months. Some of the plants are just stored while others adapted to indoor culture are grown almost as houseplants.

Regardless of climate, plants brought into the house should be given good light near a window unless you have a special setup with fluorescent lights. Keep them clear of heating ducts, and mist daily. Move plants back outdoors as soon as the weather warms up.

Ehretia buxifolia

Punica granatum

Plants

These are just a few of the plants used in tropical bonsai; read about them in the encyclopedia beginning on page 99.

Bougainvillea
Camellia sasanqua
Carissa macrocarpa (natal plum)
Casuarina equisetifolia (horsetail tree)
Ehretia buxifolia (Fukien tea)
Ficus (fig)
Fortunella (kumquat)
Podocarpus
Punica granatum (pomegranate)
Rhododendron (azalea)
Serissa foetida

Repotting

While it's possible to keep a plant in the same container for years, you'll need to prune the roots and replace the soil mix periodically to maintain the plant's health.

THE BASICS

If you left your styled tree in its nursery container, move it to a new pot after about a year. A porous container like the low clay pot pictured here, with extra drain holes drilled in it, is a good choice. The plant can remain there until you're ready to transfer it to a bonsai training pot (see pages 60–63).

A clay pot like this one forces you to begin the process of reducing the root mass to fit into increasingly shallow containers. Cutting back large roots also stimulates the growth of small feeder roots at the point of the cut.

Most plants should be repotted in early spring; tropical plants can be potted up in summer. Don't fertilize for at least a month after repotting.

1 Have your tools and soil mix ready before taking the plant out of its pot. You may have to run a spatula between the soil and pot edge to get the root ball out. If that does not work, loosen the soil around the edge with a chopstick.

2 Use chopsticks to tease the root ball and shorten it a little. With a dense mass, you might have to use a root hook (see the bottom-right photo on page 62) or even a rough-toothed saw. Remove or cut back any large, dominant roots.

3 To prevent soil from washing away, cover the pot's drain holes with plastic mesh. To secure it, fashion U-shaped staples from wire, push the ends through the mesh, and bend them back against the bottom of the pot.

4 Pull one end of a long piece of wire up through a hole on one side of the container and bring the other end up through a hole on the other side. Run another piece of wire through the same or other extra holes (depending on how many you have) so that there are four wires sticking up. These wires will be used to tie the plant into the pot.

5 Put a little soil mix in the pot (in this case, 20 percent coarse planting mix, 20 percent fine fir bark, and 60 percent red lava). Do any last-minute refinement pruning on roots before placing the plant in the pot.

6 Connect the wires with pliers: Working in a circle, bring the first wire to the second and twist it tight, then bring the end of the second to the third, and the third to the fourth. Cut a short piece of wire to connect the fourth wire back to the first.

7 Put in more potting mix, tamping it in well before adding more.

8 Water immediately with a fine spray. At first the water coming out the drain holes will look dirty or cloudy as small particles in the potting mix wash out; keep irrigating until the water runs clear.

It's Time to Repot

Here are signs that a plant needs to be repotted:

- Water won't penetrate the root mass.
- Roots are growing out the drain holes.
- The plant has lifted out of the container (because of root buildup at the bottom).
- The plant appears to be losing vigor.

CHAPTER FOUR

Taking the Next Step

NOW THAT YOU'VE GAINED some hands-on experience in bonsai, you're ready to learn new skills and tackle more challenging projects. This chapter provides information to help ease your transition from the beginner to the intermediate level. ❧ On the following pages you'll find out exactly which tools you'll need and what kind of pots to get. You'll also learn about additional classic Japanese styles—such as weeping and windswept—to add to your repertoire. Plus there are step-by-step instructions on transferring your starter plants to shallower pots and on creating deadwood. ❧ If you want to propagate certain plants instead of buying them, check the information at the end of the chapter on starting your own bonsai stock.

Tools

Get just the items you'll need to carry you through this intermediate level of bonsai. More sophisticated tools can wait until you actually require them.

TIME TO GET SERIOUS

Now that you have progressed beyond a novice, you'll want tools that allow you to work more efficiently, operate in tighter spaces, and make cleaner cuts.

Some of the implements you acquired previously, such as chopsticks, are just as useful to expert bonsaiists. But you will want to replace other items—for example, bulky side-cutting pliers in favor of more maneuverable ones, and an inexpensive turntable for a better-quality one with a stop that holds the turning surface in place while you work on a plant.

GENERAL BONSAI TOOLS The pruning and styling tools shown below include some specialized items, such as jin pliers for creating deadwood (see pages 70–71), tools for splitting and bending branches, and wire cutters for handling different sizes of wire. Long-handled

General bonsai tools useful at the intermediate level include a branch splitter (A); jin pliers (B); bending tools (C, D); a turntable with a stop (E); trimming shears (F); a large pruning saw (G); wire cutters for small wires (H); wire cutters for medium wires (I); knob cutters (J); concave cutters (K); a file for sharpening tools (L); pliers (M); and long-handled tweezers (N).

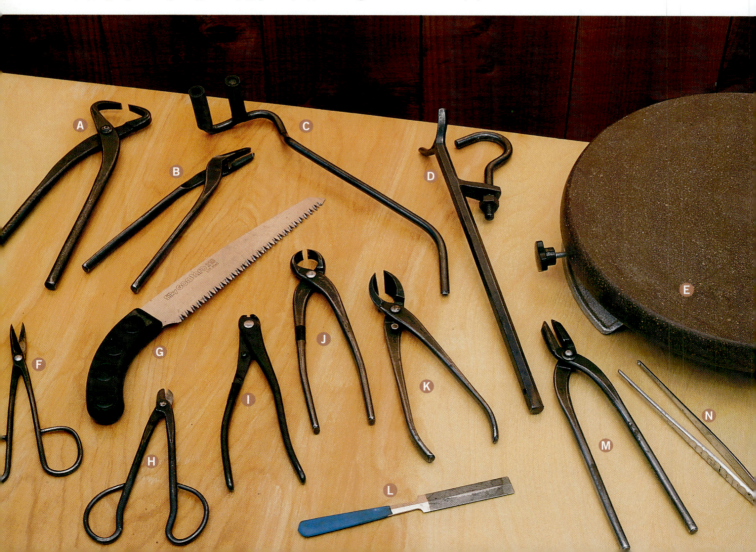

A good potting-tool collection includes soil scoops (A, B); a small broom for smoothing the potting mix (C); trowel-head tweezers for tamping down the mix (D); a two-finger rake for combing roots (E); root hooks for breaking apart root balls (F, G); chopsticks (H); plastic mesh to cover drain holes (I); a repotting sickle (J); and a sod cutter with a serrated edge (K). The last two are designed to slice through compacted root balls.

tweezers are handy for plucking conifer needles.

If you held off investing in concave cutters as a beginner, now is the time to get them. They leave a depression that calluses over nearly flat; the cut is oval-shaped. Knob cutters are a similar tool: they also leave a cupped indentation, but the cut is round. Whether you use one or the other is largely an aesthetic decision.

POTTING TOOLS Now that you will be moving starter plants into shallower training pots and

repotting periodically, it's a good idea to assemble a collection of potting tools, such as the one shown above.

Some of the tools will break apart root balls more easily than chopsticks. Others are designed for tasks such as combing roots or tamping down soil mix.

If you didn't get concave cutters before, get them now. Invaluable for severing branches and large roots, they make much closer cuts than regular garden pruners do.

Bonsai Training Pots

A few years in this type of pot prepares a plant for its ultimate destination, a formal bonsai pot (see pages 78–79). Training pots are typically a little bigger and deeper—and less expensive—than formal pots.

A TEMPORARY HOME

A plant just out of a nursery container or ordinary clay pot isn't ready to go into a formal bonsai pot just yet. Reducing its root system enough to fit a formal pot would stress the plant too much.

At this stage, the emphasis is on training the plant and not on formal presentation. Thus, a relatively inexpensive, mass-produced container—but one meant especially for bonsai training—is perfectly adequate.

Most training pots are made of clay, plastic, or mica and come in rectangular, square, oval, round, and hexagonal shapes. Pots for semicascades and cascades are deep, since the plants need the counterweight of soil to keep from toppling over.

Some pots have special features. For example, the round container in the photo at left has a large drain hole and grooves running down the inside of the pot. It is designed for training azaleas *(Rhododendron),* camellias, and other plants whose roots will rot quickly in too-wet soil.

TOP: *Bonsai training pots, such as these made from clay and plastic, tend to be fairly plain and modestly priced. This selection features rectangular, oval, and round containers in various sizes. Since the goal is visual harmony between plant and pot, your choice of container will depend on the plant's size and style.*

BOTTOM: *Some bonsai practitioners like to build wooden boxes for training large plants, such as this ponderosa pine (Pinus ponderosa).*

Positioning Plants in Pots

Here are some guidelines for achieving visual balance:

■ In a rectangular or oval container, place the plant to one side of—or atop—an imaginary horizontal line through the center. It should also be about a third of the way from one end of the pot. If the visual movement of the plant flows from left to right, place the tree on the left-hand side of the pot; if it goes from right to left, position the tree on the right-hand side. Place a slanting or windswept specimen so that the trunk leans over the center of the pot. Visual movement may be subtle in trees of other styles.

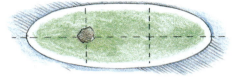

If visual movement is left to right

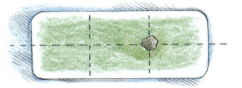

If visual movement is right to left

■ If you're planting in a round, square, or hexagonal container, center the plant—unless it's a cascade style. In that case, position the trunk slightly off-center.

■ Arrange individual trees in a grove so they fall within an asymmetrical triangle, no side of which aligns with a side of the container. The front of the planting should curve inward, to invite the viewer into the grove. Place most of the trees behind an imaginary line running horizontally through the center; position the largest tree off-center. Leave irregular spaces between individual trees and groups of trees. If the grove moves visually from left to right, leave more empty space on the right side of the container. If it flows visually from right to left, more empty space should be on the left-hand side. (See more on the grove style on page 68.)

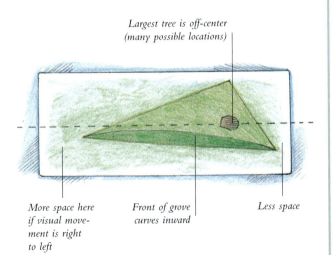

Largest tree is off-center (many possible locations)

More space here if visual movement is right to left

Front of grove curves inward

Less space

Planting in a Training Pot

After 2 or 3 years, a plant you styled as a beginner is ready to move into a bonsai training pot. Now that you have more expertise, you can start new plants in training pots rather than in nursery cans or ordinary clay pots.

If your pot has just one drain hole, use a small dowel or peg to anchor the tie-down wire. This technique works only if the pot has feet—otherwise, it will rock back and forth on the dowel.

MAKING THE MOVE

To prepare a plant for a training pot, you must bare-root it (see the step-by-step process that follows). This is true whether your plant is a new subject or a previously styled one. The best time is early spring, though tropicals can be bare-rooted in summer.

Have your tools and soil mix ready so you can pot up the plant quickly before the roots dry out. In warm climates protect the repotted plant from full sun for 2 weeks, then gradually move it to more light.

With a new subject, style it first and then bare-root it during the same session—if you feel experienced enough to see it through the extra stress. Other-wise, just plant the bare-rooted tree and wait to style the top.

Keep a plant in a training pot for around 3 years. After about a year and a half take it out, loosen the root ball, snip off any circling roots, and replant in the same pot.

1 After taking the plant out of its clay pot over a tub, use chopsticks to loosen the root ball. Clear the root crown area and check for any rot.

2 Use a root hook to dig out the old, dead roots and compacted soil on the bottom. Keep the hook away from the fresh roots on the sides.

3 Shorten long roots with scissors, then use knob cutters (pictured) or concave cutters to remove big pieces of root.

4 With the plant sitting in the tub and the old soil raked around it to protect the roots,

prepare the pot with plastic mesh and tie-down wires. See page 54 for details; since this pot has fewer drain holes, you'll need to bring two lengths of tie-down wire through each outer hole.

5 Put some soil mix in the bottom of the pot. (Equal amounts of perlite, fir bark, and red lava are shown here.) With practice, you'll be able to visually size up the root ball and figure out the right amount.

6 Gently wield chopsticks in a combing motion to clear the roots of soil. You may need to flatten the bottom a little more by snipping back the large root stubs with knob cutters or concave cutters. Use scissors to sever any overlong, crisscrossing, or dead roots.

7 After cleaning the roots by swishing them in a tub of water or hosing them off with a strong but fine spray, position the plant in the training pot. Add more potting mix.

8 Secure the plant, twisting the wire ends with pliers. See page 55 for information on connecting tie-down wires.

9 Press down and wiggle the chopsticks to push soil mix into air pockets around the roots. Smooth the soil surface with a small whisk broom. Water immediately with a fine spray; keep watering until the drainage water runs clear.

More Styles

Once you've tackled the five basic styles in the classic Japanese model (see pages 42–51), try these variations requiring somewhat more expertise.

Broom-style sawleaf zelkova (Zelkova serrata)

BROOM

This style is reminiscent of a fan-shaped Asian broom with its head pointing up. The trunk is straight and upright, with numerous slender branches creating a delicate, interlacing pattern within a mushroom- or gumdrop-shaped outline. All main branches originate from the upper part of the trunk.

In contrast with most other styles, broom plants need a large number of branches and twigs to create the desired effect. With an appropriate plant for this style, you can cut the trunk to the desired height, then encourage branches that will grow from just beneath the cut.

PLANTS Choose deciduous trees that tend to grow naturally in the desired shape, such as hackberry *(Celtis),* Chinese elm *(Ulmus parvifolia),* and sawleaf zelkova *(Zelkova serrata).*

More Sophisticated Wiring

As a beginner, you wired just the trunk and main branches. You'll still follow the same general approach explained on pages 38–40, but now you'll refine your technique.

Try handling trickier angles and wiring smaller growth—for example, from branch to branchlet.

Learn to plan ahead. Beginners tend to wire a branch, then bend it where the wire coils. Instead of letting the wire dictate the bend, practice visualizing the bend before wiring. Once you've decided where to bend, you'll know the precise points where wire should coil.

Windswept-style yew (Taxus)

WINDSWEPT

It takes little imagination to visualize a windswept bonsai. Its branches all point in one direction from a slanting trunk, as though the plant had been shaped by prevailing winds.

The trunk angle recalls the slanting style (see pages 46–47), though it may be more extreme. Branches are generally larger near the base of the plant, decreasing in size as they ascend the trunk. But regular spacing and arrangement are not the criteria for this style; your goal is to create the appearance of survival under adversity.

Because wind-battered trees frequently contain dead branches and scarred trunks, windswept bonsai are good subjects for deadwood (see pages 70–71).

Windswept trees with a strongly slanting trunk or low branches are best planted in deep pots. Those with a more upright trunk and higher branches are usually planted in shallow, sometimes wide containers.

PLANTS The trees most often associated with this style are Monterey cypress *(Cupressus macrocarpa)* and coastal species of pine *(Pinus)*. Other plants that make believable windswept specimens include juniper *(Juniperus),* larch *(Larix),* yew *(Taxus),* and hemlock *(Tsuga).*

WEEPING

Take an informal upright or slanting trunk, adorn it with pendent branches, and you have a weeping bonsai.

Branching occurs in the upper third of the trunk, with the weeping limbs rising, then arching over gracefully before descending. The weeping branches may emanate from the trunk or from short side branches. The arches should be asymmetrical to look natural.

Many specimens branch in all directions from the trunk, but others are entirely one-sided.

PLANTS The most obvious choices are naturally weeping trees, such as weeping beech *(Fagus sylvatica* 'Pendula'), tamarisk *(Tamarix parviflora),* and certain hemlock varieties like Sargent weeping hemlock *(Tsuga canadensis* 'Pendula'). You can also use non-weeping plants with some long branches that can be wired and repositioned downward—for example, the Korean hornbeam pictured below.

Weeping-style Korean hornbeam (Carpinus turczninowii)

MULTITRUNK

This style features more than one trunk originating from the same root system. These stems may rise from the soil or from an enlarged plant base. Rather than find a plant with the exact number of trunks you want, you can start with a specimen that has more, then prune off unneeded ones.

DOUBLE TRUNK One of the trunks is thicker, taller, and more dominant, bearing the more substantial branches. The two trunks initially rise together at a close angle, then gradually the smaller one moves away. If the two trunks curve, they should curve in the same direction.

Double-trunk Japanese maple
(Acer palmatum 'Ukon')

Branches are spaced much like those of formal and informal upright bonsai. The branches of the two trunks don't grow into each other, but there is no sense of separation or of one trunk repelling the other—the plant is a cohesive unit.

TRIPLE AND FIVE TRUNK The trunks should vary in thickness and height, with the largest-diameter being the tallest. The loftiest trunk usually appears slightly off-center.

Branch placement is similar to that for the double-trunk style. Regardless of the number of trunks, the composition should always look like a single plant.

CLUMP This style features a tight cluster of trunks. The sole difference from the five-trunk style is that there are more trunks.

PLANTS For multitrunk specimens, choose plants that naturally tend to branch from ground level or will send up multiple sprouts if cut close to the ground. Good choices include Japanese maple *(Acer palmatum)*, hackberry *(Celtis)*, flowering quince *(Chaenomeles)*, false cypress *(Chamaecyparis)*, haw-thorn *(Crataegus)*, holly *(Ilex)*, juniper *(Juniperus)*, crabapple *(Malus)*, olive *(Olea europaea)*, and oak *(Quercus)*.

Clump-style Hinoki false cypress
(Chamaecyparis obtusa)

Grove of Japanese beech
(Fagus crenata)

planted off-center. No two trees should be exactly the same size. For the best effect space the trees irregularly; leave uneven gaps between clusters of trees.

Depth of field and perspective are key to a good grove. Placing the largest trees in the foreground creates the sense of the forest receding from you; planting the largest trees in the background reverses the effect. (See page 61 for information on positioning a grove of trees in a container.)

PLANTS Use the same kind of tree for the whole grove, or at least similar trees with similar habits and needs. Good candidates are plants that normally grow in groves or forests, such as maple *(Acer)*, hackberry *(Celtis)*, Japanese cedar *(Cryptomeria japonica)*, beech *(Fagus)*, larch *(Larix)*, sweet gum *(Liquid-ambar)*, dwarf Alberta spruce *(Picea glauca albertiana* 'Conica'), Japanese black pine *(Pinus thunbergii)*, coast redwood *(Sequoia sempervirens)*, and bald cypress *(Taxodium distichum)*.

GROVE

This group planting consists of individual plants with separate root systems. At least five plants are needed for the proper effect, but a grove may contain dozens of trees. Use an odd number when fewer than 11 are in the composition.

The overall impression is more important than the beauty of the individual trees. You can even use trees that have defects a bit too pronounced for the plants to stand alone.

One tree in the group should be larger than the others to serve as a focal point, and it should be

Raft-style juniper (Juniperus chinensis *'Itoigawa'*)

RAFT

One of nature's clear manifestations of the will to live is the tree that falls yet remains alive to become several trees. Nourished by the root system of a downed trunk, some limbs grow upright in a small, linear grove—yet the plants are not individuals as they are in a true grove.

To create a raft, plant a tree on its side and allow select branches to become the grove. This style provides a creative use for a lopsided plant with many branches on one side but few on the other (see the illustrations below).

PLANTS Juniper *(Juniperus)* is one of the easiest raft subjects. Other candidates include flowering quince *(Chaenomeles),* cypress *(Cupressus),* pine *(Pinus),* and coast redwood *(Sequoia sempervirens).*

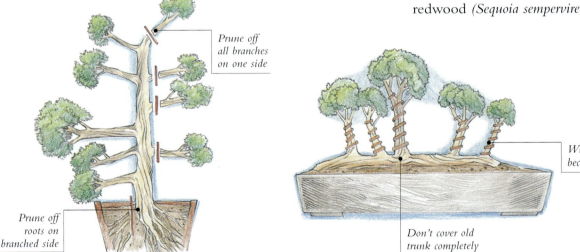

Prune off all branches on one side

Prune off roots on branched side

Wired branches become "trunks"

Don't cover old trunk completely

MAKING A RAFT

Look for a plant with a well-developed trunk and several good-size branches on one side. Cut off the branches on the other side to small stubs. Ideally, the plant will have strong roots nourishing the cut side and smaller roots feeding the branched side.

Select an odd number of irregularly spaced branches and wire them so they point generally in the same direction. You can leave some extra branches for later removal. Cut back the roots that go straight down, but leave the shorter side roots.

Position the plant on its side in a container, with the cut branch stumps down and the wired branches up. Spread out the roots in the directions you desire; cut off any that point upward. Wire the root mass into place, then cover it with potting mix. Bring the soil level up to the trunk but don't cover it.

In time the branches will develop into trunks and the planting will resemble a grove. Each of the "trees" may develop its own set of roots.

Deadwood: Jin and Shari

Artificially created deadwood can give bonsai a venerable look. The process shown here is fairly simple; see pages 86 and 87 for more elaborate examples with carved wood.

SPECIAL EFFECTS

In nature, the ravages of time and weather produce picturesque trees with dead branch snags (*jin*) and areas where trunk bark has been stripped off (*shari*). Such trees are prized by bonsai practitioners who collect plants in the wild.

These effects can be reproduced. Evergreen conifers are favorite subjects; junipers and old pines respond well and look especially convincing.

To create dead areas you cut through the bark and cambium (the green layer of growth cells under the bark), then peel back the bark to expose the woody tissue. Shari is trickier than jin because you must consider the consequences in advance. Knowing whether you can strip bark from a given area on a plant without jeopardizing certain branches comes largely with experience.

The best time of year for deadwood work is the late dormant season, prior to the start of new spring growth. Before you try these techniques on your bonsai plants, practice on cut branches of garden trees or shrubs.

TREATING DEADWOOD

Wait a few weeks for the dead areas to dry out before brushing on an undiluted solution of lime-sulfur (sold at nurseries as a dormant spray for fruit trees) to deter decay.

Since lime-sulfur dries white, some bonsaiists tone it down by adding a drop or two of India ink or dark acrylic paint to a small amount of the solution. Others prefer to let the wood discolor naturally over time.

Cover the soil mix and pot with a cloth when using lime-sulfur, to keep the solution from soaking into the root area or staining the container. Take care not to get any on live plant tissue or on yourself.

1 Shari will be created on this juniper by pulling a branch downward along the trunk and stripping off bark. Use concave cutters or knob cutters to notch the top of the branch, to make it easier to pull.

2 Hold the branch firmly while pulling downward with jin pliers. Keep tearing until the desired amount of wood has been exposed.

3 Cut the strip with scissors to taper the end and keep the tear from going too far down the trunk.

4 To jin this branch, first girdle it—press down all around the branch—with concave cutters or knob cutters.

5 Loosen the bark and cambium layer by mashing all along the branch with jin pliers. Use just enough pressure to do the job.

6 Peel the bark by hand. If it doesn't come off easily, use jin pliers.

7 A second branch on the left-hand side of the plant has also been jinned. When the exposed wood dries out, paint it with lime-sulfur. The top of the plant will be removed in a couple of years; too much green growth is counter to the concept of deadwood.

Starting Your Own Plants

Layering produces a good-size plant fairly quickly, while cuttings and seeds take longer to develop stock you can start training. For information on grafting, a more advanced technique, see page 89.

LAYERING

This technique allows you to root a branch while it's still attached to the parent plant. The success rate is high because the layered plant receives nourishment from the parent root system while it develops its own roots.

Early spring is the best time to layer plants. When the layered section is well rooted, sever the "new" plant and pot it up.

(Rooting time depends on the plant, but bonsaiists usually wait until fall to sever.)

GROUND LAYERING This works best with shrubs that branch close to the ground. A supple, low-growing stem is nicked and partially buried in the soil beneath the plant. Roots then form on the nicked portion, creating a new plant.

AIR LAYERING The principle is the same as for ground layering, but the branch is higher on the plant and the wound is covered with a moist material and then wrapped in plastic; roots will form on the wound.

By layering a stem that has branches above it, you'll have a small specimen ready for bonsai training after it's detached from the parent plant.

LEFT: *For ground layering, nick the bark of a branch near ground level where you want roots to form, dust the cut with rooting hormone, then bury the stem (held in place by a rock) in a shallow trench so that the leafy branch end points upward.*

RIGHT: *For air layering, cut a ring of bark from a pencil-thick stem. Dust the exposed area with rooting hormone, surround it with moist sphagnum moss fastened by string, then wrap with polyethylene plastic secured with electrician's tape. (Wear rubber gloves when handling sphagnum moss, which can cause a serious fungal disease in humans.)*

CUTTINGS

Except for pines and a few other conifers, most plants can be started this way. Cuttings fall into three categories, depending on the age of the wood.

Softwood (or tip) cuttings come from succulent new spring and summer growth. When bent sharply, they will usually collapse rather than snap off. These cuttings root quickly but need a moist atmosphere to prevent wilting.

Semihardwood cuttings come from growth later in summer and early fall, after stems have lengthened. They are more mature than softwood cuttings and will snap when bent.

Hardwood cuttings are from mature stems formed during the past growing season. They will spring back when bent. Many deciduous plants root easily from hardwood cuttings taken just before or during dormancy.

TAKING CUTTINGS

Make softwood and semihardwood cuttings about 6 inches long and hardwood cuttings 6 to 9 inches long. Cut straight across the stem, just below a leaf or growth bud; remove leaves from the lower half of the cutting.

Hardwood cuttings (and some semihardwood cuttings) are taken from the center portion of branches; cut on a slant just above a leaf or growth bud.

Some plants root better from a "heel cutting." This is a stem that is cut or pulled off so that it includes a small portion of the parent branch. Trim the heel with a knife so that its edges and cut surface are smooth.

With all types of cuttings, dip the bottom of the stem into a rooting hormone, then insert it into a container filled with a fast-draining medium such as a commercial seed-starting mix.

SEEDS

Choose trees and shrubs that germinate easily and grow fairly rapidly—for example, most maples *(Acer),* sweet gum *(Liquid-ambar),* and sawleaf zelkova *(Zelkova serrata).*

Seeds may be collected from plants or purchased from nurseries. Some types need special treatment like soaking, chilling, or nicking the seed coat.

Sow in flats or individual containers, using a fast-draining medium such as a commercial seed-starting mix. In cold climates, seeds are often started indoors under fluorescent lights and with bottom heat coils. Some seeds need light, and others darkness, to germinate.

Once seeds sprout, make sure that the seedlings get plenty of light, but protect them from excessive heat. Water just enough to keep the soil moist.

Various cutting types are pictured here. The plastic bag holds potted softwood cuttings in a moist environment. The small jar contains rooting hormone for coating the bottom of a cutting.

CHAPTER FIVE

Advancing Further

THE MORE YOU WORK *at developing your skills and aesthetic judgment, the further you'll progress in bonsai. You already have a few years of experience under your belt, and you're ready for more demanding projects than you undertook at the beginning and intermediate levels. You will continue with standard bonsai tasks like pruning and wiring, but now you'll be manipulating finer and finer growth.* ❧ *On the following pages, you'll find out about the kinds of tools and pots needed at this stage. You'll learn about advanced styles, including ones focusing on deadwood and others featuring exposed roots. The adventurous can consult the section on collecting plants from the wild.* ❧ *Additionally, there's information on how best to display your bonsai, both outdoors and indoors. Nowadays, bonsai are often exhibited with companion plants and viewing stones called* suiseki; *you can read about them in this chapter, too.*

What to Expect

At this point, a plant you styled as a beginner should start looking like a bonsai, especially after you move it into a formal bonsai pot (see pages 78–80). From now on, you'll devote much of your effort to refining the plant's appearance through pruning and wiring.

GOING TO THE TOP

Typically, the first 3 to 5 years of training a bonsai are spent solving root problems. During this period you are gradually reducing the size of the root ball, and you're encouraging the growth of fine roots while discouraging that of large, coarse ones.

Once you have the root system under control, you will concentrate on refining the top of the plant. This is where the artistic aspect of bonsai comes into play: balance and proportion (see page 14) are critical in creating a pleasing specimen. To evolve as a bonsaiist, you must keep developing your judgment as well as your skills.

PRUNING When you first styled a tree, you probably left certain

Pruning off the new spring growth, or "candles," on Japanese black pine (Pinus thunbergii) *and certain other pines is done yearly to encourage a denser, more compact specimen. Other plants may require different types of annual maintenance.*

branches for later removal. You may have retained some of these temporarily to nourish the tree, but you may be watching others to see how they develop. Now you'll have to decide which branches to save and which to remove. Don't rush pruning decisions if you're unsure.

Of course, the plant will keep producing new growth. Sometimes a new shoot will be better positioned than the branch originally chosen. There's nothing wrong with removing the old limb, though perhaps not until after you've developed the new one. Remember, don't stick to a preconceived plan if something develops that you like better.

WIRING Keep a sharp eye out for small growth that will add to the line and form of your bonsai; wire and shape it in the desired direction. Continue to refine your wiring technique and keep planning ahead, a process you began at the intermediate stage (see "More Sophisticated Wiring" on page 64).

Where winters are mild, you can leave deciduous trees such as this Chinese elm (Ulmus parvifolia 'Seiju') *outdoors and enjoy their silhouettes. Light pruning may be done at this time to enhance the bare structure. Any heavy pruning should wait until just before spring growth commences.*

Tools

As you pick up new techniques and refine others, you'll want to expand your tool collection. Don't go overboard; bonsai tools are somewhat like kitchen gadgets in the range and variety available. Get just the items that you know you'll use.

WHAT'S NEW?

Cutting and wiring tools in various sizes will let you handle a full range of limb and wire thicknesses. With the right-size tool, you'll avoid damaging the plant when you're pruning or snipping off wire. You'll also avoid ruining the tool by forcing it to make bigger cuts than it was designed for.

Other useful tools represent a step up in quality—for instance, stainless-steel scissors intended for bonsai instead of ordinary garden scissors. The scissors are sized perfectly for cutting twigs and buds cleanly.

Additional items are made for specialized work introduced at this level, such as grafting and defoliating. They're designed to do the job efficiently, but there's no reason you can't use an ordinary penknife with a honed edge for grafting or well-sharpened scissors for defoliating.

The tools you employed for simple deadwood work at the intermediate stage won't suffice for more extensive jins and sharis. Gravers and chisels are the usual hand tools for sculpting deadwood. If you find yourself doing a lot of deadwood work, you may want to invest in power tools for carving and polishing the wood. A selection of small paintbrushes for coating deadwood with lime-sulfur is essential.

These are among the most useful tools for advanced bonsaiists: extra-large and large knob cutters (A, B); large concave cutters (C); stainless-steel scissors (D, E); a fine saw (F); grafting knives (G); a small knife (H); gravers (I, O); large wire cutters (J); wire pliers (K); a metal brush to smooth out deadwood (L); small paintbrushes to apply lime-sulfur on deadwood (M); defoliating shears (N); chisels (P–R); and a wooden mallet (S). The mallet is used for striking a chisel when hand-carving deadwood.

Formal Bonsai Pots

However decorative a bonsai container may be, don't select it solely on the basis of how it looks on its own. The pot should be the appropriate shape, size, depth, and color to harmonize with a particular plant.

CHOOSING A POT

Proper presentation of a bonsai now becomes very important, and much more thought must go into the choice of a container than earlier in the plant's development. Formal bonsai pots represent a large step up in quality—and consequently cost—from training pots. They come in a tantalizing range of shapes, sizes, depths, colors, and materials. Some have patterns, while others are unadorned.

SHAPE Most formal bonsai pots are rectangular, square, oval, round, or hexagonal, though odd-shaped and free-form pots are also used. More choices are available within each shape than there are with training pots.

For example, some rectangular pots have soft corners, which are especially attractive with graceful deciduous trees or specimens grown for flowers or fruit. Other rectangular pots have sharp corners, to accentuate a strong,

sturdy tree. An oval pot may have flat edges or a more ornate lipped rim—one or the other may suit the plant better. A round pot with bumps along the edges to simulate a Japanese taiko drum (see pot F in the photo below) is a traditional favorite for conifers in the literati style.

Many formal pots have feet. In addition to being visually pleasing, feet elevate the pot body for better ventilation and drainage.

SIZE AND DEPTH Formal bonsai pots are available in sizes big enough to hold a grove of trees to tiny enough for miniature bonsai, *shohin.*

Pots used in earlier stages of training were deeper, to accommodate a larger root system. But since you will now be cutting back the root ball severely, you can fit a tree into a much shallower container. But just because you can get a tree into a low pot doesn't mean you should. A tree with a thick trunk wouldn't look right in a very shallow pot, while a grove of willowy trees is well suited to one.

Here are some rules of thumb to make pot selection easier. Choose a length about two-thirds the height of the plant. Look for a depth approximately equal to the thickness of the base of the trunk or the thickest trunk in

This collection of clay pots includes a handmade cascade pot (A); a glazed, soft-cornered rectangular pot (B); a sharp-cornered rectangular pot (C); an octagonal pot (D); a handmade oval pot (E); a shallow drum pot (F); a shallow, glazed, rectangular grove pot with a crackle design (G); a uniquely shaped shohin pot (H); a shallow shohin pot (I); and a handmade semicascade pot (J).

a group. (This guide-
line doesn't apply to
cascade styles, which
need tall pots as a
counterweight for the
cascading trunk.) Spacing
is a crucial element in groves;
look for a pot that is sufficiently
long and wide to allow for open
space around the planting and
between the trees (see page 61).

COLOR Most formal pots are
brown, gray, or another neutral
tone that doesn't detract from the
plant. Deciduous trees are often
planted in more vibrant containers
(blues and greens are popular) so
that the pot provides a colorful
counterpoint to the tree when it's
leafless or contrasts with the color
of berries or fall foliage.

MATERIAL Most formal bonsai
pots are made from clay; some
are mass produced and others
created individually on pottery
wheels. The more handwork,
the costlier the pot. However,
even relatively inexpensive pots
can take on an expensive-looking
patina after long exposure to
the elements.

Glazed pots are often chosen
for aesthetic reasons, but be
aware that they aren't porous.
You must pay special attention
that the roots don't become
waterlogged.

Formal pots are prone to
chips and scratches. Store them
carefully; when stacking containers
of similar sizes or shapes, place
corrugated cardboard or other
protection between them.

*A crescent moon pot sets off this blue atlas cedar (Cedrus atlantica 'Glauca').
But how do you secure the plant? You'd ordinarily use a dowel to anchor tie-down
wires through the single drain hole, but this pot has no feet and would rock on a
dowel. You could thread wires through metal mesh placed over the hole, but the
metal will rust. Some bonsaiists prefer to tape the root ball to the pot and wait
for the roots to fill out. The plant will stay in place unless pulled out.*

*The pot color serves
as a decorative accent
in winter, when
the branches of this
European beech
(Fagus sylvatica)
are bare. Because
a glazed container
like this one doesn't
"breathe," the potting
mix inside will stay
moist longer than
it would in an
unglazed pot.*

Potting Matters

Once your plant outgrows its need for a training pot, it is time to transfer it to a formal bonsai pot. To maintain the plant, repot it periodically; in years that you don't repot, top-dress the soil mix.

MOVING TO A FORMAL POT

After about 3 years in a training pot, a healthy tree is ready to move to a formal bonsai pot. See more about formal pots on pages 78–79; also consult page 61 for information on positioning plants in containers.

To plant in a formal pot, follow the same general procedures as for planting in a training pot (see pages 62–63). The main difference is you'll have to get the root mass flatter to fit a shallower pot. Use a root hook and concave cutters or knob cutters as needed to reduce the root ball to the right size. Large roots on the bottom can be cut back severely; their main function is anchorage, and you'll be tying the plant into the pot. Try to preserve as many of the small feeder roots on the sides of the root ball as you can.

If you come across a dominant root, don't remove it entirely—instead, cut it back to weaken it. New, finer roots will sprout from the cut end.

POTTING MIX Just about any mix will work in the early phases of a plant's development. Once you've advanced to this stage, be more critical about the mix you use, and gear it to the particular plant if possible.

A potting mix composed of ¼-inch chunks is standard early on. Now you may want a mix made up of ⅛-inch particles for certain plants, especially deciduous trees. Smaller particles mean smaller spaces for roots to grow, resulting in finer roots and a more finely branched top. In the case of deciduous trees, that translates to a more attractive winter silhouette. The larger particle size is still appropriate for conifers, which should look somewhat husky.

A plant's root mass must be gradually reduced to fit a shallow formal bonsai pot, but only after the trunk and roots have been allowed to develop. This robust Japanese maple (Acer palmatum 'Kiyohime') features burly trunks fanning out into thick, radiating roots that were shortened for this pot. Small feeder roots keep the plant alive and thriving.

REPOTTING

A bonsai growing in a fairly small container will need repotting more often than one in a larger pot. The frequency will depend on the pot size, plant growth habits, and length of the growing season in your area. In southern Florida, for example, a plant can produce twice the growth—including that of roots—of the same plant in a wintry climate.

Examine the soil mass to determine whether repotting is necessary. You may have to unfasten the tie-down wires and lift the plant from the container to get a good look. If you see nothing but packed roots, you'll know to repot right

away. But if you see a fair amount of soil between the roots (or soil with few roots), return the plant to its container, water it, and leave it for another year or two.

If your bonsai grows on a rock or among several rocks, you won't be able to remove it easily to examine the roots. Instead, look at the density of roots around the edges of the pot and in the drain holes.

Use the same method for repotting a bonsai as for planting it in the formal bonsai pot originally. If you've inherited

This root-bound bonsai ready for repotting came out of the pot easily, revealing a solid mass of roots with little soil.

a neglected bonsai and the plant is weak, cut back the root ball in stages: divide it into quarters and work on a single section each year.

TOP-DRESSING

Periodically removing and refreshing the top layer of potting mix will not only neaten your plants but also help keep them healthy. Among the materials you'll remove are moss, which may build up and obstruct water penetration, and weed seeds. In the photos at right, a maple *(Acer)*—currently in a larger formal pot than its eventual home—is being top-dressed.

Each year plan on top-dressing all bonsai that you're not repotting. Follow the example of veteran bonsaiists who top-dress many dozens of plants in a single session. Prepare your potting mix ahead of time and set out a few simple tools, like the ones shown here, to make the job go faster.

1 Scrape off about ¼ inch of the old potting mix along with any moss, weeds, and old fertilizer. The trowel head on these tweezers works well as a scraper. Also snip off any small roots that have accumulated in the top layer of potting mix.

2 Add new potting mix. (A combination of ⅛-inch pieces of black and red lava is used here.) Rotating the plant on a turntable makes it easier to add the mix evenly.

3 Use a small, Asian-style broom to smooth the potting mix surface.

Advanced Styles

Attempting these classic Japanese styles at the beginning or intermediate level might have proved discouraging, but now you're better prepared for the challenge. Some of the styles require baring the upper roots, and others call for extensive deadwood work.

LITERATI

This style owes its name to ancient Chinese scholars and artists (literati, or learned ones) who painted mountain landscapes depicting gaunt trees with angled trunks and sparse branches.

Well-executed literati bonsai display an almost fragile elegance. The trunk is slender, with a slight taper. Branches are few, short, irregularly placed, and spaced primarily in the upper third portion of the trunk.

In some literati, the trunk leans as much as in a slanting bonsai, but it bends or twists as though the plant had been forced to compete with neighboring trees for light. In other specimens, the trunk looks more like that of an informal upright. In both cases, sparse branches near the top of the plant clearly define it as literati.

A good artistic sense is imperative for anyone undertaking this style. There are two important things to remember about a literati bonsai: negative space is important, and less is more.

The container should be just as restrained as the plant: a very small, understated pot—usually round or slightly irregular—best suits a literati bonsai.

PLANTS The following plants will give the appropriate sparse appearance: cedar *(Cedrus)*, juniper *(Juniperus)*, larch *(Larix)*, pine *(Pinus)*, and yew *(Taxus)*.

Literati-style yew (Taxus)

EXPOSED ROOT

This style could be described as a plant on stilts. In nature such trees are sometimes found near water, growing along a stream that floods and erodes the soil around their roots.

There is no set style for trunk shape and branch placement, but avoid incongruous effects. You wouldn't expect to see a formal upright tree atop a perch of bare roots. Trunk and branch patterns modeled after slanting, semicascade, windswept, or even weeping styles will look more natural with exposed roots.

To train the long roots for this style, see below.

PLANTS You can train any plant that shows an inclination toward dramatic growth, but avoid bolt-upright trees. Good choices include pine (*Pinus*), firethorn (*Pyracantha*), and azalea (*Rhododendron*).

Exposed root–style Japanese white pine (Pinus parviflora)

TRAINING LONG ROOTS

Two bonsai styles—exposed root (see above) and root over rock (see page 84)—feature long roots, the upper portion of which are bared. You must first grow the roots to a suitable length, then acclimate them to exposure. This training process may take several years.

An easy way to train the roots is in a deep, narrow, bottomless container, such as a 1-quart or ½-gallon milk carton with the top and bottom removed. Trim the milk carton to the length you want the roots to be. Nestle the base of the carton into a broader container of potting soil, fill the carton with more soil, then plant your specimen in it.

After a year of such training, check during the plant's dormant period to see whether roots have grown down into the soil of the lower container. If they have, cut off the top few inches of the training pot and remove soil to expose the roots there. Gradually, over time, cut away more of the carton and expose more of the roots.

When the root system in the lower container appears to be sturdy enough to support the trunk and branches of your bonsai, the plant is ready for training in the exposed root or root over rock style.

*Trident maple
(Acer buergeranum)
in root over rock style*

ROOT OVER ROCK

To visualize this style, think of draping the roots of an exposed-root plant (described on page 83) over a sturdy rock protruding from a soil-filled bonsai pot. The roots form a tracery over the rock as they grow down into the soil.

The rock, with roots tenaciously clasping it, should take center stage. The upper part of the plant is a secondary player, there to enhance the root-draped stone.

Choose a rock with an interesting shape, texture, or color. You can purchase a suitable stone from a bonsai supplier or look for one outdoors; a good one may even be buried. A hard stone like granite is preferable to one that will crumble, such as sandstone or shale.

To create a root over rock composition, see the next page.

PLANTS Plants that naturally produce strong surface roots are good candidates; one of the best is trident maple *(Acer buergeranum)*. Other possibilities include Fukien tea *(Ehretia buxifolia),* pine *(Pinus),* firethorn *(Pyracantha),* azalea *(Rhododendron),* and Chinese elm *(Ulmus parvifolia).*

Peat muck

Raffia

CREATING ROOT OVER ROCK

After you've trained your plant to develop long roots (see page 83), wash the roots clean of all soil. Prune off any kinked or damaged roots; you may also want to physically separate some roots or redirect the growth of others by wiring.

Wet the stone and drape the roots over it for a close fit, making sure roots will extend into the pot. Cover the root-draped rock with "peat muck" (equal parts peat moss and clay soil, with enough water to make it the consistency of gritty modeling clay). If the roots won't cling, secure them to the rock with raffia and apply more peat muck.

Place the rock in a bonsai training pot. Partially fill the container with potting soil so that approximately one-quarter of the rock will be below the soil surface when the pot is filled. Fan out the roots that will be buried, and fill the pot with soil. You can style the top at this time.

Continued watering of the plant will gradually wash away the peat muck, leaving an exposed network of roots that will draw its sustenance from the soil in the bonsai container. Remove the raffia when you see that the roots firmly clasp the stone.

Mix and Match Styles

There's no need to stick to a single style; experiment with combinations. For example, you may want to create a grove of slanting trees, or incorporate large areas of deadwood on an informal upright bonsai. Just be sure that the combinations you choose are believable. The western hemlock (*Tsuga heterophylla*) shown here convincingly combines the windswept and three-trunk styles.

Look to nature for guidance. Also consult this book for recommended plants for each style, and check the plant encyclopedia beginning on page 99.

DRIFTWOOD

Deadwood is the focus of this style, in which extensive areas of the plant's trunk and branches are artificially weathered to look like bleached driftwood.

To style a driftwood bonsai, you create dead branch snags (jin) and stripped bark (shari) as you do in the simple deadwood work shown on pages 70–71, but on a larger, more elaborate scale. While the small areas of deadwood in the simple work serve as commentary about a plant's harsh growing conditions, deadwood on a driftwood bonsai is the plant's most prominent feature.

A driftwood bonsai may start out as a partially dead tree that has been collected from the wild. Or it may be an intact plant on which you create dead sections by using special tools like the gravers and chisels shown in the photograph on page 77.

Bonsai practitioners who are fond of working in the driftwood style often invest in a selection of power tools for carving and polishing wood. The reason for polishing the wood is to replicate the effect of nature burnishing deadwood with sand, wind, or snow.

So much of a driftwood specimen is dead that you must take special care to keep the live parts healthy. In addition to giving the plant routine care, apply lime-sulfur to the dead sections every year to prevent them from rotting.

PLANTS The best subjects are conifers. Various species of juniper *(Juniperus)* and yew *(Taxus)* are favorites because of their exceptionally hard, durable wood. Old pines also make good driftwood (the wood of young specimens is too soft); collected ponderosa pine *(Pinus ponderosa)* is a popular choice in the Midwest. Other regional favorites include American arborvitae *(Thuja occidentalis)* in the Northeast and buttonwood *(Conocarpus erectus)* in Florida; although the latter is a non-conifer, it is well adapted to this style.

Driftwood-style California juniper (Juniperus californica)

*Hollow-trunk style
pond cypress
(Taxodium ascendens)*

HOLLOW TRUNK

As with driftwood, the focus of this style is deadwood, but it is confined to a particular area. It consists of stripped bark (shari) so extensive and deep that it produces a cavity, or hollow, in the tree.

In nature, a tree may develop a hollow trunk as a result of heart rot, or strong winds or storms may have killed one side of the tree. In bonsai, you create a hollow trunk by carving, chiseling, or drilling one side of the trunk in order to interrupt the sap flow on that side. As long as the cambium (the green layer of growth cells under the bark) is intact on the other side, nutrients can flow and the tree will remain alive.

Hollow trunk is a high-maintenance style. You must be on constant alert for rot; keep it at bay by carving out any soft parts that develop and by coating the deadwood with lime-sulfur annually. Don't let moss grow on the tree; keep the hollow area exposed to sunlight and air.

PLANTS Conifers are the best candidates for this style, as they are for the driftwood style. In fact, the same trees suitable for driftwood can be given a hollow trunk. Other good subjects are bald cypress *(Taxodium distichum)* and pond cypress *(T. ascendens).* Among nonconifers, olive *(Olea europaea)* is often styled with a hollow trunk.

Defoliation

Used judiciously, this technique of snipping off all the foliage on a broad-leafed tree can promote finer branching and reduce leaf size. Try it only on very healthy trees—and not before you have full confidence in your plant-care skills.

WHY CUT OFF THE LEAVES?

The main purpose of defoliation, or leaf cutting, is providing a midseason infusion of sunlight into the center of the tree. This promotes the formation of leaf buds and more refined branching; read about ramification on page 17. Shorter internodes (spaces between leaves) and smaller leaves are by-products of this process.

Defoliation should be reserved for trees with well-established trunks and root systems. If your tree is still in an early stage of training, concentrate on developing the tree's structure before worrying about leaf size. Removing all the leaves can seriously weaken a tree or kill one that is already weak. With even a vigorous specimen, leaf cutting should not be performed 2 years in a row.

HOW TO DEFOLIATE

The best time for leaf cutting is late spring through midsummer. Be sure to do it early during this period in regions with a short growing season.

The first leaves should be somewhat mature so that the second set won't grow with greater vigor. If you remove leaves too early in spring (before the end of May), the second-growth leaves may be larger. If you wait to defoliate deciduous plants until late summer, the plant may enter dormancy early without putting out more leaves.

Snip off the entire leaf, leaving only the petiole (leaf stalk). If any portion of the leaf blade remains, the plant will concentrate its energy on maintaining the leaf fragment instead of putting out new growth.

New leaves should start to appear about 4 weeks after you remove the first set. Until new growth buds swell, keep the bonsai out of full sun but in good, filtered light. Without leaves transpiring moisture, the bonsai will need less frequent watering. Hold off on applying fertilizer while the tree is leafless.

Defoliation was employed to reduce the size of the leaves on this trident maple (Acer buergeranum). *The process is getting under way at top left, and it's partially completed at bottom left—note that the leaf stalks remain. At right, the same tree is shown with regrown foliage that is smaller and more delicate looking.*

Grafting

This advanced propagation technique involves joining a growing root system of one plant (called the stock) with a short length of stem (known as the scion) from the plant you desire. In bonsai, the less noticeable the union the better.

HORTICULTURAL SPLICING

Grafting lets you propagate plants that are difficult to root from cuttings and hard to grow from seeds. Usually it is done between two plants of the same genus—cedar to cedar, maple to maple, and so forth—but there are exceptions. Grafting is also sometimes used to add a branch for aesthetic reasons or to replace one that has died. You may even want to graft on several branches to fill out a plant interior that has become too bare.

For a graft to succeed, the cambium layers (green growth cells under the bark) of stock and scion must unite. This requires clean cuts and quick, agile handling of the wood. Veneer grafting, one of the easiest grafting techniques, is shown here.

1 Cut a pencil-thick scion from the plant you want to propagate. Trim the cut end into a tapered wedge.

2 Make a slanting cut just above the soil level into the trunk of a stock plant selected to furnish the roots.

3 Insert the wedge-trimmed stem into the slanting cut so that the cambium layers come into contact.

4 Wrap the graft with plastic grafting tape to ensure contact. In time, the top growth of the stock plant should be removed.

Collecting From the Wild

Many hobbyists take their search for good plant material on the road in the bonsai equivalent of big-game hunting. They are looking for trees dwarfed by growing in a harsh environment, such as on a mountainside, in a rock fissure, or in a bog.

THE LURE OF COLLECTING

Trees that have been dwarfed and gnarled by the elements usually make outstanding bonsai. Not only have they developed a form that speaks of their environment, but they also look old from the time you get them. Finding such a tree eliminates many years of training.

Popular collected material includes ponderosa pine *(Pinus ponderosa)* in the Midwest, bald cypress *(Taxodium distichum)* in the South, American arborvitae *(Thuja occidentalis)* in the Northeast, hemlock *(Tsuga)* in the Northwest, California juniper *(Juniperus californica)* in California and the Southwest, horsetail tree *(Casuarina equisetifolia)* in Hawaii, and buttonwood *(Conocarpus erectus)* in Florida.

TAKE CARE

Searching for plants can be dangerous, depending on where you are looking—for example, if you're on a slippery mountain slope or in a desert where flash floods may occur or scorpions are common. In such settings, bring the proper equipment (see at right), wear appropriate clothing and footwear, and don't explore on your own.

Also be sure to get permission to collect. Digging and removing plants from private and most government-owned property without consent is illegal.

WHEN TO COLLECT

Summer is a good time to dig up tropical plants, but avoid collecting temperate-climate species then. Digging temperate plants while they're dormant minimizes shock during the transplant operation.

Deciduous plants are leafless when dormant, usually fall to spring. Evergreen plants, both conifers and broad-leafed types, are generally most dormant from

This old coast live oak (Quercus agrifolia) *was collected from the wild. The bulbous lower trunks had been buried, but now they are an eye-catching feature of the tree.*

winter to early spring. The best time to dig them is shortly before they're ready to put out new growth. Though the risk is greater, you can also dig them after the new growth has firmed up, typically from late summer to early fall.

Of course, in cold-winter climates, collecting and repotting should wait until after the snow has melted.

DIGGING

Be careful how you extricate a plant—you'll have to refill the hole you make and repair any damage to the site afterward.

Start by clearing debris and other growth from beneath the plant. Prune out any unnecessary branches. To outline your dig, trace a circle on the ground around the plant; make the diameter about one-third the plant's height. For short, spreading plants, draw the circle at the tips of the branch spread.

Dig a trench just outside the circle, cutting any roots you encounter. As you sever roots, push soil over them temporarily to keep them from drying out. Free the plant by carefully digging under the root ball from all sides. Gently tilt up the root ball and lift the plant.

PROTECTING THE ROOTS

If you've dug up a sizable plant, wrap the root ball—either with the soil intact or bare-rooted with a protective cushioning of sphagnum moss—before transporting it. An experienced

A weathered California juniper (Juniperus californica) *is growing in a transition container before bonsai potting.*

collector will usually bare-root a plant, even if leafy, to make it lighter for carrying. Also, roots encased in soil are more likely to be broken apart bumping around in a vehicle.

When collecting seedlings and small plants nearby, dig leafy plants with root balls intact and temporarily pot them right away to keep the roots moist. Deciduous plants collected during their dormant season can be dug bare-root, but their roots should be kept moist until repotted.

PLANTING AND TRAINING

At home, plant the specimen as quickly as possible. Many collectors like to pot the plant in a large nursery container. Shelter the plant from wind and direct sun, and water it just enough to keep the soil moist but not soggy. Mist the foliage daily.

The new roots of winter and spring transplants should be sufficiently developed after several months so that you can place plants where they'll get sunshine. You can also begin liquid fertilizing (see page 28). Postpone feeding any summer and autumn transplants until the following spring.

Large specimens need at least a year, longer if there is little new growth, before they are disturbed again. The sign of a successful transplant is the start of healthy new growth—indicating that the plant is producing new roots. When your transplant has made a good transition, you can move it into a bonsai training pot in late winter or early spring.

Displaying Bonsai

Any work of art needs a proper showcase so that it can be appreciated to the fullest. The following pages present ideas for long-term outdoor display of your bonsai and for brief highlighting indoors. You may want to pair your bonsai with a companion plant or a viewing stone (suiseki).

OUTDOOR LIFE

If you grow just a few bonsai, you probably won't have any problem displaying them. All you need is something that elevates the pots so you can view them from the front rather than from directly overhead. A patio bench or wide deck railing, for example, will hold some plants.

But when you succumb to the allure of bonsai, you may soon find your collection outgrowing the original display space. At this point, you'll want to consider a special setup to showcase the plants.

No matter the number of bonsai you have, be sure to choose a suitable location where they will be sheltered from the elements but still receive the proper amount of light (see page 22).

TOP: *A tall stand serves as an attractive display spot for a bonsai. With this custom-made turntable affixed to the top, the stand doubles as a convenient workspace.*

LEFT: *Three shelves constructed in bleacher formation hold and display numerous plants while permitting easy access for maintenance.*

BENCHES AND SHELVES You can put together a simple bonsai bench in minutes. Select a sturdy wooden plank, such as a 2 by 12, and raise it on concrete blocks, flat stones, or other supports. If you use slats (2 by 2s or 2 by 4s) instead of a single plank, water can drain through the bench.

Another simple display unit is a set of open shelves, like a backless bookcase. Open shelves permit good air circulation and light penetration.

If you display your bonsai on shelves placed against a wall or fence, remember that heat reflection from light-colored walls can seriously damage the plants in summer. Make sure these displays

TOP: *A deck that steps up a hillside incorporates benches and shelves of varying depths and heights to accommodate a large bonsai collection. The zigzagging design adds extra interest to the display.*

BOTTOM: *A tall, narrow bench positioned against a house wall holds a collection of plants in single file. The wood shingles serve as an attractive, neutral backdrop for the bonsai.*

Built-in benches at the perimeter of a deck serve as convenient display for bonsai specimens.

TABLES Choose a table as long as desired, but just wide enough for three plants. Place the larger specimens in the middle row, flanked by smaller plants on the outside rows. Stagger placement so that no plant is directly behind another.

Or construct a unit along the lines of a patio table with attached benches. Make the center section (table) just wide enough to hold a single or double row of plants; the two lower sections (benches) can be just a bit wider to show off a number of smaller specimens.

are sheltered from direct sun during the warmest part of the day, usually late morning through afternoon.

Another effective system can be made by mounting three or four shelves like bleachers. Set the highest shelf closest to a wall or fence, the next shelf farther out, and so on. This allows water to drain freely without falling on the plants below. Don't make the shelves so deep that you can't reach the plants on top.

Staggered benches contain bonsai of all sizes in an eye-pleasing display. Many of the deciduous trees put on a colorful show in autumn (see below, left). The mild climate allows them to remain outdoors and be enjoyed all winter (see below, right).

A cascading shimpaku juniper (Juniperus chinensis sargentii) *sits elegantly on a low stand. A scroll completes the display.*

Indoor Care Tips

- Avoid moving plants in or out when the temperature differential between the outdoors and indoors is greater than 20 degrees.
- Give plants plenty of light but not direct sun.
- Keep the indoor temperature at 70°F/21°C or lower; never place plants near a heating or air-conditioning vent.
- Counteract dry indoor air with a humidifier or a pan of water placed near the bonsai.
- Thoroughly water a bonsai a few hours before bringing it indoors. If it needs more water while indoors, take it to a sink or other area where water can drain. When moving the plant, lift it carefully so the pot's feet won't scratch the furniture.

INDOOR STAY

The secrets to successfully displaying bonsai indoors are to give the plants the attention they need while in the house (see "Indoor Care Tips" at top right) and to limit the stay to a couple of days at the most.

SIMPLE DISPLAYS You may already have a table or other piece of furniture that is suitable for displaying an individual specimen. If not, try shops that specialize in Asian decor; they often carry teak and rosewood stands or low tables that work well for plant exhibit. Many sell taller, pedestal-type tables that are suitable for cascade styles.

Rather than place the bonsai container directly on the furniture, you can set it on a simple mat made of bamboo or woven natural fibers. For a rustic perch use weathered wood or a section of tree trunk; stripping off the bark and polishing the wood will lend some elegance to the perch. Another attractive option is a cut and polished slice of burled wood.

JAPANESE TOKONOMA The most formal kind of display area for bonsai is a tokonoma, a niche in a Japanese home for showcasing decorative objects. You can create your own version in an alcove or room corner.

Typically, the bonsai sits on a low table or platform, with a companion plant or viewing stone (see pages 96–97) placed nearby. A painting, a scroll, or calligraphy adorns the wall. All these objects are carefully chosen to complement each other and tell a story.

Show Time!

At some point you may want to present a prized plant in a bonsai exhibit. Typically, you just set your specimen on a table as directed by the show organizer. Although you may not have any input on the general way in which the bonsai in a show are displayed, you can do some things to improve the presentation of your individual plant.

A MOSSY CARPET

Bonsaiists exhibiting their trees often add bits of moss to the soil surface to convey the impression of a forest and to add a burst of color. The moss is usually added for the show and removed as soon as the plant is brought back home.

Less experienced hobbyists may be tempted to keep the mossy carpet full time, but that's risky. Applied too thickly it may prevent water from penetrating the soil surface; or it may retain too much water and lead to root rot or, if it touches the trunk, crown rot.

COLLECTING MOSS Advanced bonsaiists often collect their own moss. Look for the velvety moss that grows on soil or stones, not the hairlike moss that grows on tree trunks. Collecting it from places that don't have soil, such as sidewalk cracks, saves some work—otherwise, you would have to scrape away the soil since it might contain pathogens.

If you plan to use the moss patches soon, keep them moist by sealing them in plastic bags. But if you're stockpiling moss for later use, you can let it dry to a powder. Dried moss is also available at some nurseries.

APPLYING MOSS When using fresh moss, moisten the soil surface of your bonsai, then position the moss patches on top. Lightly press down to ensure contact with the soil mix. When the moss is in place, moisten it with a fine spray of water.

To use powdered moss, sprinkle it over the moistened soil surface, tamp it firmly into place, and water with a fine spray. The moss will revive if misted frequently and kept out of direct sunlight.

BONSAI COMPANIONS

Increasingly, bonsai are being exhibited with small companion plants or with viewing stones called suiseki. These items are often used in a Japanese tokonoma (see page 95), but you can utilize them in outdoor displays or more informal indoor ones.

COMPANION PLANTS Placing a small accent plant in a decorative container near a bonsai is not only aesthetically pleasing, but it's also symbolic. The companion is usually chosen to convey the season. For example, you might use a grass with browned foliage in winter, a blooming violet in spring, or a bamboo in summer.

The little companion plant can also emphasize the bonsai's place of origin. If the bonsai is an alpine species, you might choose an alpine grass to accompany it.

TOP: *Subtlety is key when using moss in a large pot: strive for little hummocks rather than a solid cover. A small trowel, like the one shown here, isn't an essential tool but it makes applying the moss easy.*

LEFT: *Clump bamboo is a favored summertime companion plant paired with bonsai.*

Many kinds of plants are suitable as companions, as long as they are naturally diminutive or can be kept little. Remember, a companion is secondary to a bonsai and should be much smaller than it. Companions are often grown in pots meant for miniature bonsai, *shohin,* but you can use any small container that has a hole for drainage.

VIEWING STONES Suiseki are natural stones evocative of outdoor scenes (such as mountains or lakes), animals, or flowers. Clubs and societies are dedicated to this ancient art form, and stones—sometimes very old and valuable ones—are displayed on their own in suiseki shows.

Now it has become popular to use viewing stones as companions for bonsai. The stone is chosen to convey something about the bonsai, such as where the bonsai is found in nature or some other symbolic information.

For example, a water-smoothed stone representing a waterfall may accompany a cascade-style bonsai. Or a stone that looks like a mountain boulder may tell you that the plant is an alpine native.

Suiseki enthusiasts will set the stone in a specially made holder that conforms to the stone's shape, but you can place it directly on the table or other display surface near the bonsai.

TOP: *Many bonsaiists who regularly exhibit their work always have on hand a selection of companion plants appropriate for their various bonsai.*

BOTTOM: *Suiseki stir the imagination, recalling images of nature. Harmonious pairings of plants and stones are increasingly a part of bonsai exhibits.*

CHAPTER SIX

Plants for Bonsai

WHILE OLD HANDS *may find almost any plant fair game for bonsai training, those with less experience will benefit from help with plant selection. The species listed in this chapter are all tried-and-true bonsai subjects.* ❧ *The listings are alphabetized by botanical name. (If you want to find a certain plant but are unsure of its scientific name, look for the common name in the index at the back of the book; the scientific name is given with it.) The information block at the top of each listing tells you whether the plant is deciduous or evergreen, the best ways to propagate it, and the ideal time to do any major pruning.* ❧ *Climate suitability is a key factor in choosing plants. A particular species may exert a powerful appeal, but do you really want it if you must struggle to keep it alive? Check the Sunset climate zones listed for a particular species to see if it's appropriate for your area; to identify your zone refer to pages 123–127.*

Abies sp.

ABIES
Fir

EVERGREEN

ZONES
vary by species

PROPAGATION
seeds, air layering

PRUNING
when buds swell in spring

In the wild, these mountain dwellers form tall pyramids of layered branches with short, stiff needles and upright cones. They are good choices for formal upright or grove training. Firs grow best in cool, moist climates and with some winter chill. Pinch new shoots throughout the growing season.

Japanese fir, *A. firma* (Zones 4–6, 15–17, 32, 34), is one of the most heat tolerant species; its needles are dark green above, lighter beneath. Korean fir, *A. koreana* (Zones 3b–9, 14–24, 32, 34, 39), produces short green needles. Alpine or Rocky Mountain fir, *A. lasiocarpa* (Zones A2, A3, 1–9, 14–17), has bluish green foliage; its variant cork fir, *A. l. arizonica* (Zones 2–9), is silvery with thick, corky bark.

ACER
Maple

DECIDUOUS

ZONES
vary by species

PROPAGATION
seeds, air layering, grafting (for named selections)

PRUNING
when buds swell in spring

New spring growth of these classic bonsai plants may be red, pink, or green; fall foliage turns yellow, orange, red, or maroon. Some selections have leaves that are bronzy red to maroon throughout the growing season. Most maples grow best where there's a bit of winter chill; leaves may burn where summers are hot and dry.

Japanese maple, *A. palmatum* (Zones A3, 2–10, 12, 14–24, 31–41), is a favorite for bonsai work. In the basic species, leaves are green with five to nine lobes. Many selections have colored leaves (red to maroon, variegated), finely dissected foliage, or colorful bark. Trident maple, *A. buergeranum* (Zones 2–9, 14–17, 20, 21, 31–41), is another favorite; its three-lobed green leaves turn red, orange, or yellow in fall. It is one of the best choices for root over rock.

Other good bonsai subjects include hedge maple, *A. campestre* (Zones 2–9, 14–17, 31–41); *A. capillipes* (Zones 2–9, 12, 14–24, 31–41); vine maple, *A. circinatum* (Zones A3, 2b–6, 14–17, 36, 37); Amur maple, *A. tataricum ginnala* (Zones A1–A3, 1–9, 14–16, 35–45); paperbark maple, *A. griseum* (Zones 2–9, 14–21, 31–41); fullmoon maple, *A. japonicum* (Zones 2–6, 14–16, 33–41); and Formosan maple, *A. caudatifolium* (Zones 5–9, 14–24, 28).

Maples adapt to various styles and are often used in groves. Make major cuts when leaf buds start to swell. Do touch-up pruning after leaves have fully expanded; remove any excessive growth, such as water sprouts, in late summer or early fall. Mature maples with overly large leaves are sometimes defoliated (see page 88).

Acer palmatum 'Deshojo'

Bougainvillea sp.

BOUGAINVILLEA

EVERGREEN

ZONES
22–27, H1, H2 (also grown, with frost protection, in 5, 6, 12–17, 19, 21, 28, 29)

PROPAGATION
softwood and semihardwood cuttings, air layering

PRUNING
spring and after flowering

This South American native is a favored plant for tropical bonsai. The plant's brilliant color (red, violet, orange, yellow, or white) comes not from the inconspicuous flowers but from the large, papery, petal-like bracts that surround them. Bloom reaches its peak in summer, but in mildest-winter areas flowers may appear from spring through fall and even into winter.

Plants lend themselves to most styles except formal upright, broom, and literati. Bougainvillea blooms on new shoots; do any major pruning after frost danger has passed and bloom is over. During the growing season, pinch back frequently to keep compact. Roots are sensitive to disturbance; don't prune them too severely.

BUXUS
Boxwood

EVERGREEN

ZONES
vary by species

PROPAGATION
softwood and semihardwood cuttings (heel cuttings work well)

PRUNING
before new spring growth

These quintessential hedge plants make handsome bonsai. Smooth wood can become thick and gnarly, a striking contrast to the small oval leaves. Pruning and regular pinching will open up plants that tend to bear dense foliage. Boxwood works well in multitrunk and informal upright styles and in groves.

Japanese boxwood, *B. microphylla japonica* (Zones 3b–24, 26–34, 39), has a poor winter appearance in frosty climates, but its variety 'Green Beauty' stays deep green in coldest weather. Another variety, 'Winter Gem' (Zones 3–24, 26–35, 37, 39), is the hardiest of Japanese boxwoods. Korean boxwood, *B. m. koreana* (Zones 2b–24, 26–41), is even hardier. 'Suffruticosa' is a slow-growing, small-leafed variety of common or English boxwood, *B. sempervirens* (Zones 3b–6, 15–17, 31–34, 39).

Buxus microphylla koreana

Camellia sasanqua

CAMELLIA sasanqua
Sasanqua

EVERGREEN

ZONES
4–9, 12, 14–24, 26–32

PROPAGATION
semihardwood cuttings, air and ground layering

PRUNING
after flowering

Glossy oval leaves are an elegant accompaniment to white, pink, or red flowers that appear in fall and early winter. Growth habit varies; some varieties are compact and upright, others spreading and almost vinelike. Those with limber, willowy stems can be trained as cascade, windswept, or, with a little more effort, weeping specimens. Choose types with small blossoms for the most pleasing look. Camellias are acid-loving plants often used in tropical bonsai.

Carissa macrocarpa

CARISSA macrocarpa
Natal plum
EVERGREEN

ZONES
22–27 (with frost protection, 12, 13, 16–21, 28)

PROPAGATION
semihardwood cuttings

PRUNING
after flowering

Used in tropical bonsai, this South African native (sometimes sold as *C. grandiflora*) is a small, upright, rounded, thorny shrub with lustrous rich green, oval, leathery leaves, and spines along branches and at twig ends. Fragrant, star-shaped white flowers are followed by small, oval, fleshy red or purple fruits.

Blooming occurs throughout the year in warmest regions; flowers, green fruit, and ripe fruit often appear together. In more temperate climates, blooms are limited to springtime. The plant is attractive as an informal upright, semi-cascade, or cascade specimen. Wire carefully since old branches can be brittle.

CARMONA microphylla
See **EHRETIA buxifolia**

CARPINUS
Hornbeam
DECIDUOUS

ZONES
vary by species

PROPAGATION
seeds, semihardwood cuttings, air layering

PRUNING
before new spring growth

Flexible stems make hornbeams easy to train as bonsai plants. Leaves are sawtooth-edged ovals that remain on plants well into autumn, turning yellow to rusty gold before dropping. Gray, furrowed bark is handsome and very hard. Species used for bonsai include European hornbeam, *C. betulus* (Zones 2–9, 14–17, 31–41); American hornbeam, *C. caroliniana* (Zones 1–9, 14–17, 26, 28–43); looseflower, *C. laxiflora* (Zones 3b–9, 14–17, 31–35, 37, 39); and Korean hornbeam,

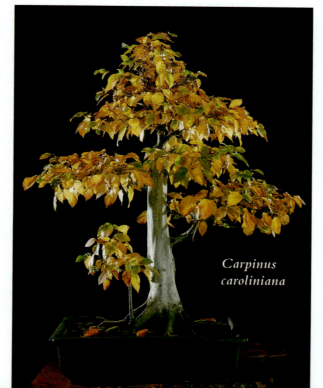

Carpinus caroliniana

C. turczninowii (Zones 3b–9, 14–17, 31–35, 37, 39).

Plants adapt to many styles. Do major pruning late in the dormant season, before the tree leafs out. Pinch excessive growth during the growing season.

Casuarina equisetifolia

CASUARINA equisetifolia
Horsetail tree
EVERGREEN

ZONES
8, 9, 12–26, H1, H2

PROPAGATION
seeds, semihardwood cuttings

PRUNING
anytime

You might mistake this Australian native and tropical bonsai favorite for a pine, but a close look at the "needles" shows that they are long, slender, jointed, gray-green branches; the true leaves are inconspicuous. Horsetail tree produces small, conelike fruit less than 1 inch long. Pendulous branches make it a good candidate for a weeping bonsai; you might also want to try slanting style.

CEDRUS
Cedar

EVERGREEN

ZONES
vary by species

PROPAGATION
air layering, grafting

PRUNING
when buds swell in spring

These stalwart skyline specimens reduce well to bonsai. Short needles come in tufted clusters; color varies from green to blue-green to nearly gray, depending on the species or variety. Stiff-needled atlas cedar, *C. atlantica* (Zones 3b–10, 14–24, 31, 32, 34), is widely used; its variety 'Glauca' has silvery blue needles. Softer needles and more flexible branches mark deodar cedar, *C. deodara* (Zones 3b–10, 14–24, 27–32, sheltered 33).

Beautiful cascade bonsai can be created with cedars; other appropriate styles include upright, slanting, literati, and multitrunk. Pinch back new shoots. Remove any cones that start to form; otherwise, the growth underneath the cone will die back. Roots can break easily, so avoid repotting too often. If your cedar is grafted, don't bend the trunk at the graft union; it may snap off.

Cedrus atlantica

Consider Native Plants

The species listed in this chapter are among the most common choices for bonsai, but not every one will be suited to your climate. Look for your Sunset climate zone in the plant listings, but also consider other plants indigenous to your area. Of course, not every native plant is a good candidate for bonsai—but if certain ones are, local bonsai practitioners and bonsai clubs probably have information about them.

Here are a couple of plants that are favorite bonsai subjects in their native ranges. Look for possibilities in your area.

CONOCARPUS ERECTUS
Florida buttonwood

ZONES
25–27, H2

This inhabitant of mangrove swamps did not actually originate in South Florida but was purportedly carried there from the West Indies by tropical storms. It is a small evergreen tree with fissured bark, light green leaves, and clusters of small, greenish to purplish flowers followed by little button-like cones. The plant is ideally suited to driftwood style.

JUNIPERUS CALIFORNICA
California juniper

ZONES
3, 6–12, 14–24

A small evergreen tree with an irregular, spreading top, this juniper has gray, shredding bark and yellowish to rich green foliage. Found on dry foothills and lower slopes of mountain ranges in most of California, western Arizona, and far southern Nevada, this species is native to more arid regions than other junipers. It is a good subject for deadwood work.

CELTIS
Hackberry

DECIDUOUS

ZONES
vary by species

PROPAGATION
seeds

PRUNING
before new spring growth

Hackberries are related to elms, displaying similar oval to lance-shaped leaves that turn yellow in autumn. Along with Chinese hackberry, *C. sinensis* (Zones 8–16,

Celtis sp.

18–20, 29–33), from eastern Asia, several North American species are available: sugarberry, *C. laevigata* (Zones 7–14, 18–20, 26, 28–35); common hackberry, *C. occidentalis* (Zones 1–24, 30–45); and western hackberry, *C. reticulata* (Zones 2–24). Other, scarcer species hail from southern Europe, western Eurasia, and the Far East.

Hackberries are suited to many styles, and they're among the handful of trees that can be trained as broom. Pinch back new growth throughout the growing season.

Chaenomeles 'Toyo Nishiki'

CHAENOMELES
Flowering quince

DECIDUOUS

ZONES
2–23, 28–41

PROPAGATION
semihardwood heel cuttings, air and ground layering, grafting

PRUNING
after flowering

Flowering quinces make showy bonsai specimens, with bright blossoms adorning otherwise bare branches from late winter to early spring. Flowers resemble single to partially double roses about 2 inches wide in white, shades of pink, orange, or red. Glossy green oval leaves are fairly small; they turn rusty yellow in autumn. Plants are usually twiggy with angular branching. They lend themselves to most styles except formal upright and broom.

CHAMAECYPARIS
False cypress

EVERGREEN

ZONES
vary by species

PROPAGATION
seeds, softwood heel cuttings, air and ground layering

PRUNING
anytime

Two species—Hinoki false cypress, *C. obtusa* (Zones A3, 2b–6, 15–17, 32–34, 36–41), and Sawara false

cypress, *C. pisifera* (Zones A3, 2b–6, 15–17, 32, 34, 38, 39)—and many varieties of both—make fine bonsai stock. Both species have dark green foliage, but needle colors in selections include blue-green, gray-green, and yellow. In general, tiny scalelike leaves are held in branching, flattened planes. Many selections carry these sprays horizontally, giving the plants a layered look. In *C. pisifera* 'Plumosa' and 'Squarossa', small, soft needles are held in feathery sprays, while several 'Filifera' varieties have threadlike twigs. False cypress cones are tiny and round.

Try any style except broom. Keep trees open and airy, since the broad foliage sprays can shade out the interior if they're too dense. Regularly pinch new growth. Don't cut back into old, leafless wood—it won't resprout.

Chamaecyparis obtusa

Corylopsis pauciflora

CORYLOPSIS
Winter hazel

DECIDUOUS

ZONES
vary by species

PROPAGATION
semihardwood cuttings, air and ground layering

PRUNING
after flowering

These acid-loving plants bear sweet-scented, bell-shaped, soft yellow flowers that hang in short, chainlike clusters on bare branches in early spring. Buttercup winter hazel, *C. pauciflora* (Zones 4–7, 14–17, 31–34), has clusters of 2 or 3 flowers; spike winter hazel, *C. spicata* (Zones 3b–7, 14–17, 31–39), produces 6 to 12 flowers in a cluster. Toothed, nearly round leaves follow; foliage is tinged pink when young, then turns bright green. Fall leaf color varies from none to poor to a good clear yellow.

Plants are often trained as single- or multiple-trunk informal upright specimens, but other styles are possible.

COTONEASTER
EVERGREEN, SEMIEVERGREEN, AND DECIDUOUS

ZONES
vary by species

PROPAGATION
seeds, semihardwood heel cuttings, air and ground layering

PRUNING
before new spring growth and after berries fade

Plants range from upright shrubs and shrub-trees to spreading ground covers. All feature small white or pinkish flowers (like tiny single roses) in spring, and red to orange pea-size berries in autumn. Deciduous types offer orange to red fall foliage.

The best bonsai subjects are found among the small-leafed, low-growing species. Evergreen kinds include *C. buxifolius* (Zones 4–24, 31), *C. congestus* (Zones 3b–24, 31–39), *C. dammeri* (Zones 2–24, 29–41), and *C. microphyllus* (Zones A3, 2–9, 14–24, 31–41). *C. salicifolius* 'Repens' (Zones 3b–24, 31–34, 39) is evergreen or semievergreen. Among the deciduous types are *C. adpressus* (Zones 2–24, 29–41), *C. apiculatus* (Zones A3, 2–24, 29–43), and *C. horizontalis* (Zones A3, 2b–11, 14–24, 31–41). Cotoneasters are suited to most styles except formal upright and broom.

Cotoneaster dammeri 'Streib's Findling'

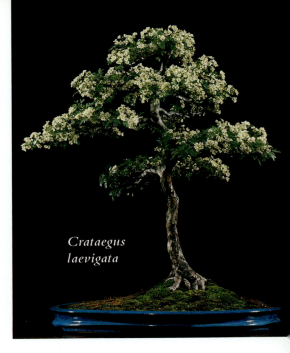

Crataegus laevigata

CRATAEGUS
Hawthorn

DECIDUOUS

ZONES
vary by species

PROPAGATION
seeds

PRUNING
before new spring growth

These twiggy, thorny trees provide all-season interest: tiny white or pink flowers in spring; red fruits in summer; yellow, orange, or red leaves in fall; and an attractive bare branch structure in winter.

Most species have lobed leaves; cockspur thorn, *C. crus-galli* (Zones 2–12, 14–17, 28, 30–41), and carriere hawthorn, *C.* × *lavallei* (Zones 3–12, 14–21, 29–35, 37, 39), have toothed, oval leaves. The toothed, lobed leaves of English hawthorn, *C. laevigata* (Zones 2–12, 14–17, 28, 30–41), typically have poor fall color. *C. cuneata* (Zones 3b–9, 14–17, 32, 34) is shrubby with small lobed leaves. Hawthorns lend themselves to almost any style except formal upright and broom.

Cryptomeria japonica

CRYPTOMERIA japonica
Japanese cedar

EVERGREEN

ZONES
4–9, 14–24, 32–34, 39

PROPAGATION
softwood heel cuttings, air and ground layering

PRUNING
anytime

This Japanese timber tree has several dwarf variants suitable for bonsai work; the most widely available is 'Elegans', sometimes called plume cedar. Soft-textured needles to 1 inch long densely clothe branches. Grayish green during the growing season, they change to coppery purple in cold weather. This species is a good candidate for upright and slanting styles; plants also make good groves. Shoots have a tendency to turn brown and die back. Dense growth will need periodic pruning and pinching, which can be done anytime. Don't pinch back to old growth or the branchlet may die off.

CUPRESSUS
Cypress

EVERGREEN

ZONES
vary by species

PROPAGATION
seeds

PRUNING
anytime

Cypresses are conifers that produce tiny, scalelike leaves closely set on cordlike branches. Arizona cypress, *C. arizonica* (Zones 7–24, 26–31), may have green, blue-gray, or silvery leaves. It has rough, furrowed bark, while its variant *C. a. glabra* has smooth, cherry red bark. Monterey cypress, *C. macrocarpa* (Zones 5, 6, 14–17, 21–24), which has bright green leaves, spreads picturesquely in age, especially in windy coastal areas.

Cypresses are suited to upright, slanting, semicascade, and windswept styles, and grove and raft training. Prune anytime, especially before the spring growth flush; nip back new shoots throughout the growing season.

Cupressus macrocarpa

Ehretia buxifolia

EHRETIA buxifolia (CARMONA microphylla)
Fukien tea

EVERGREEN

ZONES
25, H2

PROPAGATION
seeds, softwood cuttings

PRUNING
anytime

A mainstay of tropical bonsai, Fukien tea thrives indoors. Glossy, dark green foliage like that of boxwood (*Buxus*) densely clothes the branches; the bark is light brown and becomes fissured with age. Tiny white flowers borne throughout the year are followed by red berries. The plant is a favorite for *penjing*. It also lends itself to most traditional Japanese styles; its tiny leaves and fine branching structure make it a good choice for miniature bonsai, *shohin*. Pinch back new growth regularly.

ELAEAGNUS

EVERGREEN AND DECIDUOUS

ZONES
vary by species

PROPAGATION
softwood cuttings

PRUNING
before new spring growth

These fast-growing, tough plants are tolerant of heat and wind. Foliage is distinguished in evergreen forms by silvery dots, which reflect sunlight; in evergreen silverberry, *E. pungens* (Zones 4–24, 26–33), the dots are rust-colored. Deciduous forms have silvery leaves; those of *E. multiflora* (Zones 2b–24, 28–41) are silvery green above, silvery brown below. Tiny, usually fragrant spring flowers of elaeagnus are followed by decorative fruit, typically red with silvery flecks. Plants are suited to most styles except formal upright and broom. Pinch throughout the growing season.

EUONYMUS

DECIDUOUS

ZONES
vary by species

PROPAGATION
seeds, semihardwood cuttings

PRUNING
before new spring growth

Several species offer vivid, reddish pink fall foliage plus orange to red, usually squarish fruits that open to reveal orange seeds. Corky ridges on stems distinguish winged euonymus, *E. alatus* (Zones A3, 2–10, 14–16, 29–45), from smooth-stemmed spindle bush, *E. europaeus* (Zones 1–9,

Elaeagnus pungens

14–16, 31–45); strawberry bush, *E. americanus* (Zones 3b–9, 14–17, 26, 28, 30–34, 39); and wahoo, *E. atropurpurea* (Zones 2–9, 14–16, 28, 31–43).

Euonymus alatus

Plants are suited to most styles except broom; try capitalizing on their naturally angular growth by training them in single- or multiple-trunk slanting, windswept, or cascade styles.

FAGUS
Beech

DECIDUOUS

ZONES
vary by species

PROPAGATION
seeds, grafting (for named selections)

PRUNING
before new spring growth

With their massive trunks and domed canopies, beeches possess an air of majesty and are often choices for park plantings. As bonsai, they offer sturdy, smooth-barked trunks and fairly symmetrical branching. Leaves turn brown in autumn, remaining on stems well into winter. Attractive brown, pointed leaf buds highlight the winter silhouette. Remove the old brown leaves then—they detract from the leaf buds and keep sunlight from penetrating the inner part of the tree. Pull each leaf backward, away from the new leaf bud; if you pull

Fagus crenata

in the direction of the bud, you may pull off the bud as well.

The most common species is European beech, *F. sylvatica* (Zones A3, 2b–9, 14–21, 32–41). Many named selections are available, including those with bronze and purple foliage, deeply cut leaves, and weeping branches. Less widely available are American beech, *F. grandifolia* (Zones 1–6, 31–43), and Japanese beech, *F. crenata* (Zones 2b–6, 32–41). Train types

with pendent branches as weeping bonsai. Others are best trained in upright or slanting styles; they also make effective groves. Wire carefully: the wood is brittle.

FICUS
Fig

EVERGREEN	
ZONES	*vary by species*
PROPAGATION	*softwood cuttings, air layering*
PRUNING	*anytime*

Figs are among the most popular trees for tropical bonsai. Of the hundreds of species and varieties in the world, some of the most often used in bonsai are willow-leaf fig, *F. neriifolia* (Zones 15–17, 19, 21–26, H1, H2); and Indian laurel fig or Chinese banyan, *F. microcarpa,* also sold as *F. retusa* (Zones 9, 13, 16–25, 27, H1,

H2). These and other species that form aerial roots are often trained naturally with a spreading canopy or in a freeform shape with aerial roots featured. Figs are also suited to most traditional Japanese styles except literati. Cut back new shoots throughout the year. Figs exude a white milky sap when pruned.

FORSYTHIA

DECIDUOUS	
ZONES	*A2, A3, 2b–11, 14–16, 18, 19, 30–41*
PROPAGATION	*softwood and semihardwood cuttings*
PRUNING	*after flowering*

Forsythia viridissima 'Bronxensis'

In nature these are fountain-shaped shrubs whose bare branches are covered with yellow blossoms in early spring. As bonsai, they look a little coarse and are grown mainly for their flowers. Forsythia looks good as a clump or cascade, although other styles are possible. Cut back hard after bloom is over, then keep pinching until midsummer, when the following year's flower buds are formed. *F. viridissima* 'Bronxensis' is a slow-growing dwarf form.

Ficus microcarpa

FORTUNELLA
Kumquat

EVERGREEN

ZONES
8, 9, 12–29, H1, H2

PROPAGATION
grafting

PRUNING
after frost danger is past

A favorite for tropical bonsai, kumquat is actually among the cold-hardiest of citrus, withstanding temperatures to at least 18°F/−8°C when grown in the ground. Its many attributes include glossy leaves, fragrant white flowers in spring, and yellow to red-orange fruits like tiny oranges in fall or winter.

Kumquat is best suited to regions with warm to hot summers and chilly nights during fruit ripening. Plants don't grow well on their own roots and

Fortunella margarita 'Nagami'

so are usually grafted, often onto trifoliate orange, grapefruit, or sour orange stock. Try any style except broom or literati. Do any major pruning only after frost danger is over; do any touch-up pruning after harvest (unless frost is expected soon). Pinch back new growth as it is produced.

GINKGO biloba
Maidenhair tree

DECIDUOUS

ZONES
A2, A3, 1–10, 12, 14–24, 28, 30–44

PROPAGATION
seeds, semihardwood and hardwood cuttings

PRUNING
before new spring growth

Bright green leaves have the shape of a scalloped fan—just like the leaflets of maidenhair fern. Spectacular autumn color is a bright butter yellow to gold. A naturally erect habit in maturity suggests training in an upright style. Ability to sprout from the base also makes ginkgo a good candidate for clump training. Additionally, this plant is often trained in groves. It is best grown as a fairly large specimen since the leaves don't easily reduce in size. Male varieties are most commonly used; their leaves usually have a deep cleft on the scalloped edge, an attractive feature when viewed close-up.

Ginkgo biloba

What Kind of Plant?

These are terms used to describe woody plants—the trees and shrubs grown in gardens and as bonsai.

BROAD-LEAFED *Plant with wide leaves. Usually used in reference to broad-leafed evergreens, to distinguish them from needled evergreens, or conifers. Many produce showy flowers or fruit.*

CONIFER *Plant with needlelike or scalelike leaves; bears seeds in cones (like pinecones) or modified conelike structures (like juniper berries).*

DECIDUOUS *Any plant that sheds all its leaves annually, usually in autumn. Most are broad-leafed, but a few are conifers, such as bald cypress (Taxodium distichum).*

EVERGREEN *Any plant that has leaves throughout the year.*

SEMIEVERGREEN *Any plant that tends to be evergreen in mild-winter areas but deciduous in colder ones.*

HAMAMELIS
Witch hazel

DECIDUOUS	
ZONES	*vary by species*
PROPAGATION	*air and ground layering, grafting*
PRUNING	*after flowering*

These sometimes treelike shrubs have a spreading habit and angular or zigzag branches. As garden plants they're appreciated for red, purple, and yellow fall foliage and nodding clusters of yellow to red blooms that

Hamamelis × intermedia 'Pallida'

appear in winter or early spring. As bonsai they're grown for their flower display; their large leaves and rangy growth habit don't make them ideal bonsai subjects in other seasons. The spectacular blossoms consist of many narrow, crumpled petals that are said to resemble shredded coconut, mop heads, or spiders. The flowers are scented in some species. Choices include *H. × intermedia,* a group of hybrids (Zones 3–7, 15–17, 31–34, 39); Japanese witch hazel, *H. japonica* (Zones 2b–7, 15–17, 31–34, 39); and Chinese witch hazel, *H. mollis* (Zones 2b–7, 15–17, 31–34, 39). Try growing all types as informal upright specimens.

ILEX
Holly

EVERGREEN AND DECIDUOUS	
ZONES	*vary by species*
PROPAGATION	*semihardwood cuttings*
PRUNING	*spring, summer*

As bonsai, hollies are primarily grown for foliage and not berries. Hollies with large, spiny foliage are less favored than those with small leaves, spiny or plain. Most species bear female and male flowers on separate plants; a nearby male plant is needed for the female to produce berries.

Among evergreen species, Japanese holly, *I. crenata* (Zones 3–9, 14–24, 28, 31–35, 37), has little leaves that resemble those of boxwood *(Buxus)* and produces black berries; yaupon, *I. vomitoria* (Zones 4–9, 11–26, 28, 31, 32, H1, H2), also has boxwoodlike foliage and will produce red berries without a pollinator nearby. Deciduous *I. serrata* (Zones 2b–9, 14–21, 31–41) bears slightly larger, narrower, thin-textured leaves that color well before falling and produces red berries. These hollies make good upright and multi-trunk specimens; they are also suited to miniature bonsai, *shohin.*

JUNIPERUS
Juniper

EVERGREEN	
ZONES	*vary by species*
PROPAGATION	*softwood and semihardwood cuttings, air and ground layering*
PRUNING	*spring, summer*

Junipers are virtually the perfect bonsai plants. They're tough, malleable, long-lived, and fine textured. Good specimens can originate from cuttings, but among the most beautiful examples of bonsai art are gnarled old junipers collected from the wild. Age—or the appearance of it—suits these plants; deadwood seems to be a natural component of mature specimens.

Ilex vomitoria

Juniperus horizontalis

Junipers have two kinds of foliage: juvenile leaves are short, prickly needles, while mature foliage consists of tiny overlapping scales.

Almost any juniper can be trained as a bonsai. With more than 60 species plus countless selections, there is a vast pool of material. Some are naturally upright and treelike; others are shrubs and ground covers. Blue-green *J. procumbens* 'Nana' (Zones 1–24, 28–43), a dwarf ground cover, is a good choice for beginners; it is well suited to slanting and cascade styles. Creeping juniper, *J. horizontalis* (Zones 1–24, 31–45; some varieties can also be grown in A1–A3, 28), may be styled many ways, including as a raft (see the photo above). Shimpaku, *J. chinensis sargentii,* also known as *J. sargentii* (Zones A2, A3, 1–24, 26, 28–44), lends itself to all styles except broom. Eastern red cedar, *J. virginiana* (Zones A3, 1–24, 26, 28, 31–43), a conical tree in nature, is amenable to most styles except cascades and broom; its dark green foliage turns reddish in cold weather.

Major pruning can be performed anytime, although it is best done in spring or summer. Don't cut back into leafless wood on old junipers or new growth may not occur. Pinch junipers regularly.

LAGERSTROEMIA indica
Crape myrtle

DECIDUOUS

ZONES
4–10, 12–24, 25–31, warmer 32

PROPAGATION
seeds, semihardwood and hardwood cuttings

PRUNING
before new spring growth

Bark is a special feature—smooth and gray, flaking to reveal pink patches beneath. Plants may bear clusters of papery white, pink, red, or purple flowers at the ends of shoots in summer. Small oval leaves become incandescent orange-red in autumn.

Crape myrtle adapts to informal upright, slanting, and multi-

Lagerstroemia indica

trunk styles. Pinch regularly to encourage a network of fine branches, but be careful not to remove all the flower buds if blossoms are desired. You can do touch-up pruning after flowering is over.

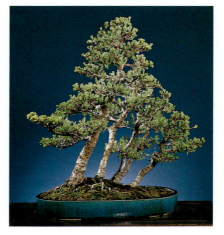

Larix laricina

LARIX
Larch

DECIDUOUS

ZONES
vary by species

PROPAGATION
seeds

PRUNING
just before needles emerge

Larches are among the few needle-leafed plants that lose their foliage each fall (see also *Metasequoia* and *Taxodium*). Fresh apple green, new spring growth matures to needles about 1 inch long, which turn gold or russet in autumn and then drop. Tiny roundish cones are typically purplish. Most species, including American larch, *L. laricina* (Zones A1–A3, 1, 2, 37–45), prefer cool summers and chilly winters. Japanese larch, *L. kaempferi* (Zones 1–9, 14–19, 32, 34,

36–45), is more tolerant of warm, mild conditions.

Natural growth of larches is rigidly upright, making them suitable for upright forms and groves. You can also try slanting, windswept, and literati styles. Do any major pruning in spring, after the green leaf buds form but before the needles emerge—the buds are among larch's most attractive features. New growth will sprout from cuts made into leafless stems.

LIQUIDAMBAR

Sweet gum

DECIDUOUS

ZONES
vary by species

PROPAGATION
seeds, softwood cuttings, air layering

PRUNING
before new spring growth

From their lobed leaves, you might mistake these trees for maples, and the vivid colors of their autumn foliage reinforce that similarity. American sweet gum, *L. styraciflua* (Zones 3–9, 14–37, 39), is a tall, fairly slender tree with leaves having five to seven lobes; fall foliage color is purple, yellow, or red. Oriental sweet gum, *L. orientalis* (Zones

Malus × micromalus

5–9, 14–24, 26, 28, 31, 32), is a shorter tree with smaller leaves that are deeply five lobed, each lobe again lobed to give a lacy effect; fall color varies from deep gold and bright red in cooler areas to dull brown-purple in warmer winter climates.

Naturally erect sweet gums are well suited to upright styles and groves. Because they will sprout from the base, you can also create multitrunk specimens. Pinch regularly.

MALUS

Crabapple

DECIDUOUS

ZONES
1–11, 14–21, 29–43

PROPAGATION
seeds

PRUNING
before new spring growth

These miniature apples present the maximum seasonal change in

regions where they get winter chill. Springtime brings a floral display; autumn offers yellowish foliage; and small fruits decorate the branches from late summer into winter. Numerous species and named selections (some extra cold-hardy) are available, but several stand out for bonsai training.

Japanese flowering crabapple, *M. floribunda,* has white blooms opening from red to pink buds; small fruits are yellow and red. Sargent crabapple, *M. sargentii,* is white flowered (pink in the form 'Rosea') with tiny red fruits. Midget crabapple, *M. × micromalus,* is a slow grower with red buds opening to pink flowers; fruit is red or greenish.

Crabapples are suited to a variety of styles, including informal upright, slanting, and multitrunk. Pinch back overlong shoots after bloom is over.

Liquidambar orientalis

METASEQUOIA glyptostroboides
Dawn redwood

DECIDUOUS

ZONES
A3, 3–10, 14–24, 31–41

PROPAGATION
seeds, semihardwood and hardwood cuttings

PRUNING
anytime

Short green needles and upright growth suggest evergreen coast redwood *(Sequoia sempervirens),* but these needles turn bronzy brown in autumn, then drop. New spring foliage is light green. The bark is a thick, fibrous orange-brown.

Dawn redwood is a natural for groves and appropriate for upright and slanting styles. Plants can be pruned anytime, but before new spring growth emerges is an especially good time. Pinch throughout the growing season.

Olea europaea

OLEA europaea
Olive

EVERGREEN

ZONES
8, 9, 11–24, H1, H2

PROPAGATION
semihardwood cuttings, air and ground layering

PRUNING
anytime

Olive performs best where winters are mild and summers fairly dry. Plants have smooth gray bark and narrow, deep green leaves with silvery undersides. 'Little Ollie' is a dwarf variety that has small leaves.

The natural tendency of olives is to grow a number of trunks, making them suitable for training as multitrunk bonsai.

Other styles, including hollow trunk, are also seen. New growth sprouts freely from the base; remove all unwanted shoots as they appear.

Metasequoia glyptostroboides

PICEA
Spruce

EVERGREEN

ZONES
vary by species

PROPAGATION
seeds, air layering

PRUNING
when buds swell in spring

Spruces have upright trunks, tiers of regularly spaced branches, and a conical shape. Short needles densely cover branches, spiraling around them in bottlebrush fashion; cones hang down. Most species come from northern latitudes or high altitudes, making them poor subjects where winters are mild and summers warm to hot.

Yeddo spruce, *P. jezoensis* (Zones A3, 2–7, 14–17, 34, 36–41), has green and silver needles that remain less than 1 inch in length; its variant, *P. j. hondoensis,* has even shorter needles and a more compact growth habit. The light green tufts of new growth in spring are as decorative as any floral display. Dwarf Alberta spruce, *P. glauca albertiana* 'Conica' (Zones A2, A3, 1–7, 14–17, 32–45), is a slow-growing, compact pyramid with ¾-inch-long needles that put on a "flowery" show of new growth similar to that of Yeddo spruce. Colorado blue spruce, *P. pungens glauca* (Zones A2, A3, 1–10, 14–17, 32–45), is grown for its bluish foliage. Engelmann spruce,

Picea engelmanii

P. engelmanii (Zones A2, A3, 1–7, 10, 14–17), resembles blue-green forms of *P. pungens,* but its needles are softer and the tree is not as wide at the base.

Erect symmetry makes spruces natural candidates for upright styles and groves; slanting and multitrunk are other apt styles. Don't cut back to leafless branches, as new growth won't sprout. When pinching, leave some new growth.

PINUS
Pine

EVERGREEN	
ZONES	
vary by species	
PROPAGATION	
seeds, air layering	
PRUNING	
when buds swell in spring	

Pines are among the classic bonsai plants. Although native to many climates and locales, they are also associated with the trying natural conditions producing weather-ravaged plants that serve as models for several bonsai styles. Pines can be trained in upright, slanting, literati, windswept, and multitrunk styles. They're also suitable for grove, raft, exposed root, and root over rock plantings; even cascades are possible. Old pines are good deadwood subjects.

You can train practically any pine as bonsai, but the most effective specimens usually are created from species with shorter needles, such as Japanese black pine, *P. thunbergii* (Zones 3–12, 14–21, 26, 28–37, 39); Japanese white pine, *P. parviflora* (Zones 2–9, 14–24, 32–41); mugho pine,

P. mugo mugo (Zones A1–A3, 1–11, 14–24, 32–45); and Scotch pine, *P. sylvestris* (Zones A1–A3, 1–9, 14–21, 32–45). In the Pacific Coast region, shore pine, *P. contorta contorta* (Zones A3, 4–9, 14–24, H1), and Monterey pine, *P. radiata* (Zones 14–24, H1), are favorites. In the Southwest, try several piñon pines: *P. cembroides* (Zones 2–24), *P. edulis* (Zones 1–11, 14–21), and *P. monophylla* (Zones 2–12, 14–21). In cold-winter northern and eastern regions, good choices are jack pine, *P. banksiana* (Zones A1–A3, 1, 2, 34, 37–45); Japanese red pine, *P. densiflora* (Zones 2–9, 14–17, 32–41, H1); Swiss mountain pine, *P. mugo uncinata* (Zones A1–A3, 1–11, 14–24, 32–45); ponderosa pine, *P. ponderosa* (Zones 1–10, 14–21, 35, 41, 43, H1); and eastern white pine, *P. strobus* (Zones 1–6, 32–45).

Make hard cuts in spring as buds swell (but hold off until fall in the case of Japanese white pine because its sap bleeds profusely in spring). New growth in spring appears as "candles" at the tip of each branch. For the greatest increase in plant size, leave the candles alone or prune them partway back.

Different pines require different pruning techniques. For example, on Japanese black pine, remove candles at their points of origin and style only with the new growth that sprouts from those points later that year or the next year. Cut the candles before needles start to elongate.

On all pines, thin out excessive growth and old needles in fall. Don't cut back into bare wood on mature trees (more than about 15 years old); new growth won't sprout.

Pinus thunbergii

Podocarpus macrophyllus maki

PODOCARPUS

EVERGREEN

ZONES
vary by species

PROPAGATION
softwood cuttings, air layering

PRUNING
anytime

Leaves generally resemble those of related yews *(Taxus),* but in most species they are longer, broader, and lighter in color. Plants are often used in tropical bonsai. They're suitable for most classic Japanese styles except broom. Pinch regularly.

Heat-tolerant yew pine or southern yew, *P. macrophyllus* (Zones 4–9, 12–28, 31, H1, H2), has fairly limber branches. Its variant shrubby yew pine, *P. m. maki,* is slower growing and smaller. *P. nagi* (Zones 8, 9, 14–28, H1, H2) has pendulous branchlets. *P. nivalis* (Zones 4–9, 14–17), a dwarf species used for bonsai in the West, has short, dark olive green needles like those of yews. Fine-textured fern pine, *P. gracilior* (Zones 8, 9, 13–25, southern 26, 27, H1, H2), grows well in dry climates.

PRUNUS
Flowering apricot, flowering plum

DECIDUOUS

ZONES
vary by species

PROPAGATION
seeds, air layering

PRUNING
before new spring growth

Flowers—and, to a lesser extent, fruits—are special features of the many deciduous *Prunus* species grown for ornamental purposes. Bonsai favorites include several Asian species.

The earliest to flower (from middle to late winter) is Japanese flowering apricot, *P. mume* (Zones 3–9, 12–22, 31–34, 39). Small, single pink blossoms later produce yellow fruits up to 1 inch in diameter. This is perhaps the longest-lived *Prunus* species; it becomes picturesque and gnarled with age.

Flowering plums bloom between mid-winter and midspring. Myrobalan or cherry plum, *P. cerasifera* (Zones 3–22, 28, 31–34, 39), has small white blossoms that are followed by cherry-size red fruits. Purple-leaf plum, *P. ×*
blireana (Zones 3–22, 32–34, 39), has foliage that emerges reddish purple, then turns greenish bronze by summer; it produces pink to red flowers and no fruit.

These species can be trained many ways, but they are especially suited to styles that emphasize or accommodate irregularity. Hard pruning should be done before new spring growth commences, but it will sacrifice spring flowers. Cut back strong shoots in summer, taking care not to remove flowering wood. Pinch back new growth as it is produced.

Prunus × blireana

Pseudocydonia sinensis

PSEUDOCYDONIA sinensis
Chinese quince

DECIDUOUS OR SEMIEVERGREEN

ZONES
3–10, 14–21, 30–34, 39

PROPAGATION
hardwood cuttings, air and ground layering

PRUNING
before new spring growth

The bark is reason enough to grow this tree: it flakes off to reveal a patchwork of brown, green, and gray. Roundish oval, dark green leaves turn a good yellow and red in fall. The plant pro- duces a scattering of pale pink flowers to 1½ inches wide in spring. Be prepared to prune early in the year, since the tree is among the first to leaf out. Pinch off spent flowers if you don't want huge, egg-shaped fruits. The plant is a good choice for single- or multiple-trunk infor- mal upright or slanting styles.

PUNICA granatum
Pomegranate

DECIDUOUS

ZONES
5–31, warmer 32, H1, H2

PROPAGATION
semihardwood cuttings

PRUNING
after flowering or fruiting

This Mediterranean native is a popular choice for tropical bonsai. Narrow leaves emerge bronzy and age to glossy bright green; in autumn they turn yellow before dropping. Showy flowers in summer or early fall develop into fruits in some varieties.

Small-growing selections are best for bonsai: 'Chico' has red-orange blos- soms resembling carnations; 'Nana' bears single orange flowers followed by small, dull red fruits; and 'Nejikan' features a twisted trunk. Pomegranates can be trained with a single trunk or with multiple trunks in most styles except formal upright and broom.

PYRACANTHA
Firethorn

EVERGREEN

ZONES
vary by species

PROPAGATION
seeds, semihardwood cuttings, air and ground layering

PRUNING
after fruiting

With naturally angular growth, firethorns make picturesque bonsai specimens. Narrow, dark green leaves appear on stems with needlelike thorns. Clusters of tiny white blossoms in spring mature into pea- size fruits that turn red, orange, or yellow in fall. Species used for bonsai include *P. angustifolia* (Zones 3–24, 29–35, 37, 39), a Chinese native, and the similar *P. coccinea* (Zones 3–24, 26, 28–39), from the eastern Mediterranean; both are best known for their varieties.

Pyracantha sp.

Firethorn's growth habit suggests training in irregular styles, especially slanting, windswept, and cascade. Other styles to try are multitrunk, informal upright, exposed root, and root over rock.

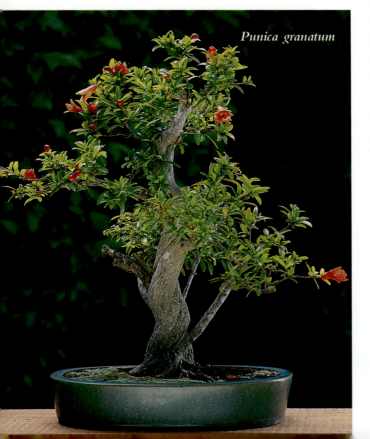

Punica granatum

Quercus suber

QUERCUS
Oak

EVERGREEN AND DECIDUOUS

ZONES
vary by species

PROPAGATION
seeds

PRUNING
before spring growth

Oaks make fine bonsai; their heavy trunks and gnarled branches suggest majesty on a small scale. The best species are those with relatively small leaves. Among evergreens, these include coast live oak, *Q. agrifolia* (Zones 7–9, 14–21), and many other California and Oregon natives; kermes oak, *Q. coccifera* (Zones 7–9, 14–24); holly or holm oak, *Q. ilex* (Zones 4–24, warmer 32); cork oak, *Q. suber* (Zones 5–16, 18–24); and southern live oak, *Q. virginiana* (Zones 4–31). Choices are more limited among deciduous species: valley oak, *Q. lobata* (Zones 3b–9, 12–24), and English oak, *Q. robur* (Zones A2, A3, 1–12, 14–21, 32–43), have 3- to 4-inch leaves.

Oaks lend themselves to informal upright and multitrunk styles; a naturalistic style is becoming popular. Pinch regularly.

RHODODENDRON
Azalea

EVERGREEN

ZONES
vary by species and hybrids

PROPAGATION
semihardwood cuttings, air and ground layering

PRUNING
before flowering

These acid-loving plants are easy to train, growing freely and sprouting new growth anywhere you make a cut. Older plants develop thick, gnarled trunks and major branches. And you get a blossom display in the bargain. Proportion is the chief concern: you want plants that have small leaves and flowers. This can be a problem, since most azaleas have been developed for large, showy blossoms. The best bonsai candidates are found among the Kurume hybrids (Zones 5–9, 14–24, 28, 31, H1, H2) and Satsuki hybrids (Zones 5–9, 14–24, 28, 31, warmer 32 and 33); the latter may be sold as Macrantha hybrids. A nursery specializing in rhododendrons and azaleas may reveal other small-foliage species and hybrids worth trying.

Informal upright and multi-trunk are styles to which azaleas adapt easily. Also try cascades, exposed root, and root over rock. With careful training, even broom is possible. Plants are also used in tropical bonsai.

At first cut off all flower buds so that energy will go into trunk and branch development; after 3 or 4 years, you may let the plant blossom. You can prune hard before bloom, but for best flowering don't do it every year.

Rhododendron
Satsuki hybrid

Sequoia sempervirens

SEQUOIA sempervirens
Coast redwood

EVERGREEN

ZONES
4–9, 14–24, warmer 32

PROPAGATION
semihardwood cuttings, burls

PRUNING
when buds swell in spring

This plant's ramrod-straight trunk is covered in cinnamon-colored, shredding bark. Leaves appear almost delicate in contrast: narrow and needlelike, carried in flattened sprays. They emerge bright light green in spring and darken as they mature. The upright trunk and a relatively narrow branch spread make this a good choice for formal upright training as well as for grove and raft plantings. Cut to the ground, a plant will send up a number of shoots that you may select for multitrunk training.

When pruning branches, you can cut back to bare wood; new growth will sprout. Pinching new growth is important since branch tips grow quickly. Also rub off excessive buds along the trunk, at the base of the tree, and in branch crotches.

SERISSA foetida

EVERGREEN

ZONES
5–9, 14–32

PROPAGATION
softwood and semihardwood cuttings

PRUNING
after flowering

A staple of tropical bonsai, this lovely small shrub has a densely branched, somewhat angular form covered with a profusion of tiny, glossy green leaves (about ¼ to ½ inch long). In some varieties the leaves are variegated. Small, funnel-shaped blossoms are scattered over this backdrop from spring to autumn; they can be white or pink, single- or double-flowered.

With its rather angular branching habit, serissa adapts to such styles as slanting and windswept; it can also be trained in most other styles except formal upright and broom. It is well suited to miniature bonsai, *shohin*. Regularly pinch back leggy growth.

STEWARTIA monadelpha

DECIDUOUS

ZONES
4–6, 14–17, 20, 21, 31–33

PROPAGATION
softwood cuttings

PRUNING
before new spring growth

This slow-growing tree with slender, upward-angled branches is an all-season performer. It has fresh green leaves in spring, white flowers like single camellias in summer, and bright red foliage in fall. In winter a distinctive

Serissa foetida

Stewartia monadelpha

pattern of bare branches and attractive caramel-colored, pointed leaf buds are on display. The bark is rich brown and scaly when young, cinnamon-colored and smooth when older. Stewartia is attractive in upright styles and groves. Plants appreciate acid conditions.

TAMARIX parviflora
Tamarisk

DECIDUOUS

ZONES
2–24, 28–43

PROPAGATION
semihardwood and hardwood cuttings, air layering

PRUNING
after flowering

Often sold as *T. africana* or *T. tetrandra,* this is typically a graceful, arching shrub with tiny leaves that produce a feathery effect. Profuse flowers are pink at first, turn tan, and then brown. Tamarisk species are difficult to classify, leading to much confusion. Some species, including *T. parviflora,* bloom in early spring on wood produced the previous year; they should be pruned after bloom. Other types bloom in late spring or summer on new shoots. No matter what name is on the nursery label, if your

Tamarix parviflora

tamarisk is a late bloomer, prune in the late dormant season.

Tamarisk is best trained in a weeping style. Every year new growth that has hardened off must be wired to create a weeping form. Older wood can also be wired during winter dormancy; do it gently or the wood will break. Plants can be difficult to handle because of their long tap root and brittle wood.

TAXODIUM distichum
Bald cypress

DECIDUOUS

ZONES
2–10, 12–24, 26, 28–43

PROPAGATION
seeds, semihardwood cuttings

PRUNING
before new spring growth

Bald cypress is valued for its cinnamon-colored, shaggy bark and graceful sprays of short, narrow, flat, needlelike leaves. The tree is pyrami-

dal in youth, then develops a wide-spreading top. Its needles turn rusty brown in autumn and drop, leaving a bare winter silhouette. In nature, the trunk is buttressed near the base, and when growing in waterlogged soil it develops knobby growths called knees. It has traditionally been trained in a formal upright style, but a natural flat-top style is becoming popular. It is also well suited to hollow trunk style and groves. Regular pinching and rubbing off excessive budding are necessary.

Pond cypress, *T. ascendens* (Zones 4–9, 12–24, 26, 28–41), is similar in most details but is narrower and more erect, and its trunk is not as strongly buttressed. It lends itself to the same styles and demands the same attention to pinching as bald cypress.

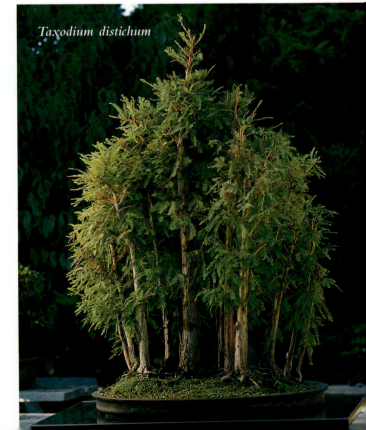

Taxodium distichum

TAXUS
Yew

EVERGREEN

ZONES
vary by species

PROPAGATION
semihardwood cuttings, air layering

PRUNING
anytime

Yews have narrow, flat, needlelike leaves arranged in a spiral around branches; their bark is reddish brown and peeling. They are darker green, more formal looking, and more tolerant of shade and moisture than most conifers. And instead of cones, female plants produce fleshy, scarlet, berrylike fruit. The plants most often trained as bonsai are English yew, *T. baccata* (Zones A3, 3–9, 14–24, 32, 33, warmest 34), and Japanese yew, *T. cuspidata* (Zones A2, A3, 2–6, 14–17, 32–41).

Taxus baccata 'Aurea'

Yew looks good as an informal upright, slanting, windswept, or literati bonsai. Cutting back or bending large branches is difficult because the wood is so hard; however, hardness makes yew a good candidate for incorporating deadwood. You can cut back to bare wood; new growth will sprout. Pinch new shoots regularly, but wait until after bloom if you want fruit.

THUJA occidentalis
American arborvitae, white cedar

EVERGREEN

ZONES
A2, A3, 1–9, 15–17, 21–24, 32–45, H1, H2

PROPAGATION
semihardwood heel cuttings

PRUNING
anytime

This Northeastern native needs moist air to look its best. Mature foliage consists of flat sprays that are bright green to yellowish green, turning brown in severe cold. The basic species is seldom offered at nurseries, but smaller garden varieties are common. Some are naturally pyramidal or columnar, others globe-shaped. 'Emerald' has a narrow cone shape and green foliage that holds its color all winter.

American arborvitae can be trained in most styles except broom. Because this species grows in very cold northern regions, deadwood can be incorporated to indicate its harsh environment. Don't cut back to a bare branch; it won't sprout new shoots.

Thuja occidentalis

Ulmus parvifolia 'Seiju'

TSUGA
Hemlock

EVERGREEN	
ZONES	*vary by species*
PROPAGATION	*seeds, air layering*
PRUNING	*anytime*

Although they grow as upright cones of foliage, hemlocks aren't stiff. Soft, short needles (less than 1 inch long) grow densely on arching to drooping branchlets.

All hemlocks need humidity for good growth. The best species for cool-summer regions of the Pacific Coast are western hemlock, *T. heterophylla* (Zones A2, A3, 2–7, 14–17), and mountain hemlock, *T. mertensiana* (Zones A1–A3, 1–7, 14–17). For warmer summer temperatures in the northeastern and mid-Atlantic regions, the best choices are Canada hemlock, *T. canadensis* (Zones A3, 2–7, 17, 32–43); Carolina hemlock, *T. caroliniana* (Zones 4–6, 32–41); and Japanese hemlock, *T. sieboldii* (Zones 3b–7, 15–17, 32, 34, 37, 39).

All styles except broom are suitable. New growth will sprout if you cut back to bare wood.

Tsuga mertensiana

ULMUS parvifolia
Chinese elm

DECIDUOUS OR SEMIEVERGREEN	
ZONES	*3–24, 26–35, 37–39*
PROPAGATION	*softwood cuttings, air and ground layering*
PRUNING	*before new spring growth*

Of the numerous elm species, Chinese elm is perhaps the best for bonsai. It's a fast grower with limber branches that bear oval leaves to 2 inches long. In mild winters, foliage is partially to totally evergreen. Especially favored are smaller-leafed selections, such as 'Seiju' and 'Hokkaido', which have leaves to ¼ inch long and bark that becomes corky with age. Multitrunk and broom styles take advantage of Chinese elm's natural growth habit; also try root over rock. The plant grows so fast that constant pinching is necessary to maintain a fine network of branches.

VITIS
Grape

DECIDUOUS	
ZONES	*vary by species and variety*
PROPAGATION	*hardwood cuttings, ground layering*
PRUNING	*before new spring growth*

The many varieties of these vines have lobed, sometimes toothed, leaves that turn color in fall. As the trunk ages, it can become attractively gnarled.

Vitis sp.

Plants don't dwarf well, so plan on a large bonsai. Among grapes suited to your climate (check local nurseries), look for types with relatively small leaves and small fruit. Plants adapt well to cascades and can also be trained as informal uprights. For good fruiting, prune canes back to two or three buds in the dormant season.

WISTERIA

DECIDUOUS	
ZONES	*vary by species*
PROPAGATION	*air layering*
PRUNING	*before flowering*

Wisteria's glory is its spectacular spring display of sweet pea–like blossoms in long, pendent clusters. Foliage is quite lush and large, consisting of numerous oval to lance-shaped leaflets per leaf. Because of flower cluster and leaf sizes, wisteria is best grown as a medium or large specimen.

Wisteria floribunda

The most common species, Chinese wisteria, *W. sinensis* (Zones 3–24, 26, 28–35, 37–39), has foot-long clusters of flowers on bare wood. Both Japanese wisteria, *W. floribunda* (Zones 2–24, 26, 28–41), with the longest floral clusters, and silky wisteria, *W. brachybotrys* (Zones 3–24, 32–35, 37, 39), with the shortest ones, blossom after leaves have emerged. American wisteria, *W. frutescens* (Zones 28–34), blooms even later.

Grow wisteria in a style that shows off the flowers: slanting, weeping, or multitrunk, with spreading branches so flowers hang like a curtain. Plants are vigorous vines that need a lot of pruning and pinching to stay within bounds and put on a good flower display. Make hard cuts before bloom, do any touch-up pruning after bloom, and cut back long tendrils at the end of summer. Plants raised from seed will take many years to flower; air layering produces a blooming specimen faster.

ZELKOVA serrata
Sawleaf zelkova

DECIDUOUS	
ZONES	*3–21, 28–35, 37, 39*
PROPAGATION	*seeds, air layering*
PRUNING	*before new spring growth*

The natural growth habit of sawleaf zelkova is in the form of a broom—many branches splaying upward and outward from nearly the same point atop the trunk. Naturally, this tree is a favorite for the broom style of bonsai. Its overall appearance suggests an elm but with beechlike smooth, gray bark that becomes flaky in old specimens. The 2- to 3-inch-long, oval, serrated leaves turn yellow, red, or reddish brown in fall.

Prune branches as needed during the dormant season, keeping in mind the aesthetics of the winter silhouette. Pinch regularly during the growing season to maintain twigginess. A mature specimen with over-large leaves can be defoliated (see page 88).

Zelkova serrata

SUNSET'S GARDEN CLIMATE ZONES

A plant's performance is governed by the total climate: length of growing season, timing and amount of rainfall, winter lows, summer highs, humidity. *Sunset*'s climate zone maps take all these factors into account—unlike the familiar hardiness zone maps devised by the U.S. Department of Agriculture, which divide the U.S. and Canada into zones based strictly on winter lows. The U.S.D.A. maps tell you only where a plant may survive the winter; our climate zone maps let you see where that plant will thrive year-round. Below and on pages 124–125 are brief descriptions of the zones illustrated on the maps on pages 125–127. For more information, consult *Sunset*'s regional garden books.

ZONE 1A. Coldest Mountain and Intermountain Areas in the West
Growing season: mid-June to early Sept. All zone is west of Continental Divide, with mild days, chilly nights. Average lows to −0°F/−18°C, extreme lows to −40°F/−40°C; snow cover (or winter mulch) key to perennials' success.

ZONE 1B. Coldest Eastern Rockies and Plains Climate
Growing season: mid-May to late Sept. All zone is east of Continental Divide, with warm days, warmer nights than 1A. Summer rainfall present, wind a constant. Winter arctic cold fronts create sudden temperature shifts; average lows to 0°F/−18°C, extreme lows to −50°F/−46°C.

ZONE 2A. Cold Mountain and Intermountain Areas
Growing season: mid-May to mid-Sept. Occurs at lower elevation than Zone 1A; summers are mild, winters to 10°F/−12°C (extremes to −30°F/−34°C) with snow. The coldest zone for growing sweet cherries, hardiest apples.

ZONE 2B. Warmer-summer Intermountain Climate
Growing season: mid-May to Oct. Premier fruit- and grain-growing climate with long, warm to hot summers. Winters to 12°F/−11°C (extremes to −20°F/−29°C) with snow.

ZONE 3A. Mild Areas of Mountain and Intermountain Climates
Growing season: May to mid-Oct. Long, dry, warm summers favor a variety of warm-season crops, deciduous fruits, many ornamentals. Occurs at higher elevation the farther south it is found. Winter temperatures drop to 15°F/−9°C with extremes to −18°F/−28°C; snow is possible.

ZONE 3B. Mildest Areas of Intermountain Climates
Growing season: early April to late Oct. Compared with Zone 3A, summers are warmer, winters milder: to 19°F/−7°C with extremes to −15°F/−26°C. Snow is possible. Excellent climate for vegetables, also a wide variety of ornamentals that prefer dry atmosphere.

ZONE 4. Cold-winter Western Washington and British Columbia
Growing season: early May to early Oct. Summers are cool, thanks to ocean influence; chilly winters (19° to −7°F/−7° to −22°C) result from elevation, influence of continental air mass, or both. Coolness, ample rain suit many perennials and bulbs.

ZONE 5. Ocean-influenced Northwest Coast and Puget Sound
Growing season: mid-April to Nov., typically with cool temperatures throughout. Less rain falls here than in Zone 4; winter lows range from 28° to 1°F/−2° to −17°C. This "English garden" climate is ideal for rhododendrons and many rock garden plants.

ZONE 6. Oregon's Willamette Valley
Growing season: mid-Mar. to mid-Nov., with somewhat warmer temperatures than in Zone 5. Ocean influence keeps winter lows about the same as in Zone 5. Climate suits all but tender plants and those needing hot or dry summers.

ZONE 7. Oregon's Rogue River Valley, California's High Foothills
Growing season: May to early Oct. Summers are hot and dry; typical winter lows run from 23° to 9°F/−5° to −13°C. The summer-winter contrast suits plants that need dry, hot summers and moist, only moderately cold winters.

ZONE 8. Cold-air Basins of California's Central Valley
Growing season: mid-Feb. through Nov. This is a valley floor with no maritime influence. Summers are hot; winter lows range from 29° to 13°F/−2° to −11°C. Rain comes in the cooler months, covering just the early part of the growing season.

ZONE 9. Thermal Belts of California's Central Valley
Growing season: late Feb. through Dec. Zone 9 is located in the higher elevations around Zone 8, but its summers are just as hot; its winter lows are slightly higher (temperatures range from 28° to 18°F/−2° to −8°C). Rainfall pattern is the same as in Zone 8.

ZONE 10. High Desert Areas of Arizona, New Mexico, West Texas, Oklahoma Panhandle, and Southwest Kansas
Growing season: April to early Nov. Chilly (even snow-dusted) weather rules from late Nov. through Feb., with lows from 31° to 24°F/−1° to −4°C. Rain comes in summer as well as in the cooler seasons.

ZONE 11. Medium to High Desert of California and Southern Nevada
Growing season: early April to late Oct. Summers are sizzling, with 110 days above 90°F/32°C. Balancing this is a 3½-month winter, with 85 nights below freezing and lows from 11° to 0°F/−12° to −18°C. Scant rainfall comes in winter.

ZONE 12. Arizona's Intermediate Desert
Growing season: mid-Mar. to late Nov., with scorching midsummer heat. Compared with Zone 13, this region has harder frosts; record low is 6°F/−14°C. Rains come in summer and winter.

ZONE 13. Low or Subtropical Desert
Growing season: mid-Feb. through Nov., interrupted by nearly 3 months of incandescent, growth-stopping summer heat. Most frosts are light (record lows run from 19° to 13°F/−7° to −11°C); scant rain comes in summer and winter.

ZONE 14. Inland Northern and Central California with Some Ocean Influence
Growing season: early Mar. to mid-Nov., with rain coming in the remaining months. Periodic intrusions of marine air temper summer heat and winter cold (lows run from 26° to 16°F/−3° to −9°C). Mediterranean-climate plants are at home here.

ZONE 15. Northern and Central California's Chilly-winter Coast-influenced Areas
Growing season: Mar. to Dec. Rain comes from fall through winter. Typical winter lows range from 28° to 21°F/−2° to −6°C. Maritime air influences the zone much of the time, giving it cooler, moister summers than Zone 14.

ZONE 16. Northern and Central California Coast Range Thermal Belts
Growing season: late Feb. to late Nov. With cold air draining to lower elevations, winter lows typically run from 32° to 19°F/0° to −7°C. Like Zone 15, this region is dominated by maritime air, but its winters are milder on average.

ZONE 17. Oceanside Northern and Central California and Southernmost Oregon
Growing season: late Feb. to early Dec. Coolness and fog are hallmarks; summer highs seldom top 75°F/24°C, while winter lows run from 36° to 23°F/2° to −5°C. Heat-loving plants disappoint or dwindle here.

ZONE 18. Hilltops and Valley Floors of Interior Southern California
Growing season: mid-Mar. through late Nov. Summers are hot and

dry; rain comes in winter, when lows reach 28° to 10°F/–2° to –12°C. Plants from the Mediterranean and Near Eastern regions thrive here.

ZONE 19. Thermal Belts around Southern California's Interior Valleys

Growing season: early Mar. through Nov. As in Zone 18, rainy winters and hot, dry summers are the norm—but here, winter lows dip only to 27° to 22°F/–3° to –6°C, allowing some tender evergreen plants to grow outdoors with protection.

ZONE 20. Hilltops and Valley Floors of Ocean-influenced Inland Southern California

Growing season: late Mar. to late Nov.—but fairly mild winters (lows of 28° to 23°F/–2° to –5°C) allow gardening through much of the year. Cool and moist maritime influence alternates with hot, dry interior air.

ZONE 21. Thermal Belts around Southern California's Ocean-influenced Interior Valleys

Growing season: early Mar. to early Dec., with same tradeoff of oceanic and interior influence as in Zone 20. During winter rainy season, lows range from 36° to 23°F/2° to –5°C—warmer than Zone 20, since colder air drains to the valleys.

ZONE 22. Colder-winter Parts of Southern California's Coastal Region

Growing season: Mar. to early Dec. Winter lows seldom fall below 28°F/–2°C (records are around 21°F/–6°C), though colder air sinks to this zone from Zone 23. Summers are warm; rain comes in winter. Climate here is largely oceanic.

ZONE 23. Thermal Belts of Southern California's Coastal Region

Growing season: almost year-round (all but first half of Jan.). Rain comes in winter. Reliable ocean influence keeps summers mild (except when hot Santa Ana winds come from inland), frosts negligible; 23°F/–5°C is the record low.

ZONE 24. Marine-dominated Southern California Coast

Growing season: all year, but periodic freezes have dramatic effects (record lows are 33° to 20°F/1° to –7°C). Climate here is oceanic (but warmer than oceanic Zone 17), with cool summers, mild winters. Subtropical plants thrive.

ZONE 25. South Florida and the Keys

Growing season: all year. Add ample year-round rainfall (least in Dec. through Mar.), high humidity, and overall warmth, and you have a near-tropical climate. The Keys are frost-free; winter lows elsewhere run from 40° to 25°F/4° to –4°C.

ZONE 26. Central and Interior Florida

Growing season: early Feb. to late Dec., with typically humid, warm to hot weather. Rain is plentiful all year, heaviest in summer and early fall. Lows range from 15°F/–9°C in the north to 27°F/–3°C in the south; arctic air brings periodic hard freezes.

ZONE 27. Lower Rio Grande Valley

Growing season: early Mar. to mid-Dec. Summers are hot and humid; winter lows only rarely dip below freezing. Many plants from tropical and subtropical Africa and South America are well adapted here.

ZONE 28. Gulf Coast, North Florida, Atlantic Coast to Charleston

Growing season: mid-Mar. to early Dec. Humidity and rainfall are year-round phenomena; summers are hot, winters virtually frostless but subject to periodic invasions by frigid arctic air. Azaleas, camellias, many subtropicals flourish.

ZONE 29. Interior Plains of South Texas

Growing season: mid-Mar. through Nov. Moderate rainfall (to 25" annually) comes year-round. Summers are hot. Winter lows can dip to 26°F/–3°C, with occasional arctic freezes bringing much lower readings.

ZONE 30. Hill Country of Central Texas

Growing season: mid-Mar. through Nov. Zone 30 has higher annual rainfall than Zone 29 (to 35") and lower winter temperatures, normally to around 20°F/–7°C. Seasonal variations favor many fruit crops, perennials.

ZONE 31. Interior Plains of Gulf Coast and Coastal Southeast

Growing season: mid-Mar. to early Nov. In this extensive east-west zone, hot and sticky summers contrast with chilly winters (record low temperatures are 7° to 0°F/–14° to –18°C). There's rain all year (an annual average of 50"), with the least falling in Oct.

ZONE 32. Interior Plains of Mid-Atlantic States; Chesapeake Bay, Southeastern Pennsylvania, Southern New Jersey

Growing season: late Mar. to early Nov. Rain falls year-round (40" to 50" annually); winter lows (moving through the zone from south to north) are 30° to 20°F/–1° to –7°C. Humidity is less oppressive here than in Zone 31.

ZONE 33. North-Central Texas and Oklahoma Eastward to the Appalachian Foothills

Growing season: mid-April through Oct. Warm Gulf Coast air and colder continental/arctic fronts both play a role; their unpredictable interplay results in a wide range in annual rainfall (22" to 52") and winter lows (20° to 0°F/–7° to –18°C). Summers are muggy and warm to hot.

ZONE 34. Lowlands and Coast from Gettysburg to North of Boston

Growing season: late April to late Oct. Ample rainfall and humid summers are the norm. Winters are variable—typically fairly mild (around 20°F/–7°C), but with lows down to –3° to –22°F/–19° to –30°C if arctic air swoops in.

ZONE 35. Ouachita Mountains, Northern Oklahoma and Arkansas, Southern Kansas to North-Central Kentucky and Southern Ohio

Growing season: late April to late Oct. Rain comes in all seasons. Summers can be truly hot and humid. Without arctic fronts, winter lows are around 18°F/–8°C; with them, the coldest weather may bring lows of –20°F/–29°C.

ZONE 36. Appalachian Mountains

Growing season: May to late Oct. Thanks to greater elevation, summers are cooler and less humid, winters colder (0° to –20°F/–18° to –29°C) than in adjacent, lower zones. Rain comes all year (heaviest in spring). Late frosts are common.

ZONE 37. Hudson Valley and Appalachian Plateau

Growing season: May to mid-Oct., with rainfall throughout. Lower in elevation than neighboring Zone 42, with warmer winters: lows are 0° to –5°F/–18° to –21°C, unless arctic air moves in. Summer is warm to hot, humid.

ZONE 38. New England Interior and Lowland Maine

Growing season: May to early Oct. Summers feature reliable rainfall and lack oppressive humidity of lower-elevation, more southerly areas. Winter lows dip to –10° to –20°F/–23° to –29°C, with periodic colder temperatures due to influxes of arctic air.

ZONE 39. Shoreline Regions of the Great Lakes

Growing season: early May to early Oct. Springs and summers are cooler here, autumns milder than in areas farther from the lakes. Southeast lakeshores get the heaviest snowfalls. Lows reach 0° to –10°F/–18° to –23°C.

ZONE 40. Inland Plains of Lake Erie and Lake Ontario

Growing season: mid-May to mid-Sept., with rainy, warm, variably humid weather. The lakes help moderate winter lows; temperatures typically range from –10° to –20°F/–23° to –29°C, with occasional colder readings when arctic fronts rush through.

ZONE 41. Northeast Kansas and Southeast Nebraska to Northern Illinois and Indiana, Southeast Wisconsin, Michigan, Northern Ohio

Growing season: early May to early Oct. Winter brings average lows of −11° to −20°F/−23° to −29°C. Summers in this zone are hotter and longer west of the Mississippi, cooler and shorter nearer the Great Lakes; summer rainfall increases in the same west-to-east direction.

ZONE 42. Interior Pennsylvania and New York; St. Lawrence Valley

Growing season: late May to late Sept. This zone's elevation gives it colder winters than surrounding zones: lows range from −20° to −40°F/−29° to −40°C, with the colder readings coming in the Canadian portion of the zone. Summers are humid, rainy.

ZONE 43. Upper Mississippi Valley, Upper Michigan, Southern Ontario and Quebec

Growing season: late May to mid-Sept. The climate is humid from spring through early fall; summer rains are usually dependable. Arctic air dominates in winter, with lows typically from −20° to −30°F/−29° to −34°C.

ZONE 44. Mountains of New England and Southeastern Quebec

Growing season: June to mid-Sept. Latitude and elevation give fairly cool, rainy summers, cold winters with lows of −20° to −40°F/ −29° to −40°C. Choose short-season, low heat-requirement annuals and vegetables.

ZONE 45. Northern Parts of Minnesota and Wisconsin, Eastern Manitoba through Interior Quebec

Growing season: mid-June through Aug., with rain throughout; rainfall (and humidity) are least in zone's western part, greatest in eastern reaches. Winters are frigid (−30° to −40°F/−34° to −40°C), with snow cover, deeply frozen soil.

ZONE A1. Alaska's Coldest Climate—Fairbanks and the Interior

Growing season: mid-May to early Sept. Summer days are long, mild to warm; permafrost usually recedes below root zone. Winter offers reliable snow cover. Season extenders include planting in south and west exposures, boosting soil temperature with mulches or IRT plastic sheeting. Winter lows drop to −20°F/−29°C, with occasional extremes to −60°F/−51°C.

ZONE A2. The Intermediate Climate of Anchorage and Cook Inlet

Growing season: mid-May to mid-Sept. Climate is moderated by mountains to the north and south, also by water of Cook Inlet. Microclimates reign supreme: winter lows may be 5°F/−15°C but with extremes of −40°F/−40°C possible. Summer days are cool to mild and frequently cloudy.

ZONE A3. Mild Southern Maritime Climate from Kodiak to Juneau

Growing season: mid-May to Oct. Summers are cool and cloudy, winters rainy and windy. Typical lows are to 18°F/−8°C with extremes to −18°F/−28°C. Winter-spring freeze-thaw cycles damage plants that break growth early. Cool-weather plants revel in climate but annual types mature more slowly than usual.

ZONE H1. Cooler Volcanic Slopes from 2,000 to 5,000 Feet

Found only on Hawaii and Maui, this zone offers cooler air (and cooler nights) than lower Zone H2; temperatures here are better for low-chill fruits (especially at higher elevations) and many non-tropical ornamentals. Warm-season highs reach 65° to 80°F/19° to 27°C; cool-season lows drop to around 45°F/7°C.

ZONE H2. Sea Level to 2,000 Feet: the Coconut Palm Belt

The most heavily populated region in the islands, this has a tepid climate with high temperatures in the 80° to 90°F/27° to 32°C range, low temperatures only to about 65°F/18°C. Rainiest period is Nov. through March, the remaining months, on leeward sides, being relatively dry. Windward sides of islands get more precipitation than leeward sides from passing storms and year-round tradewind showers.

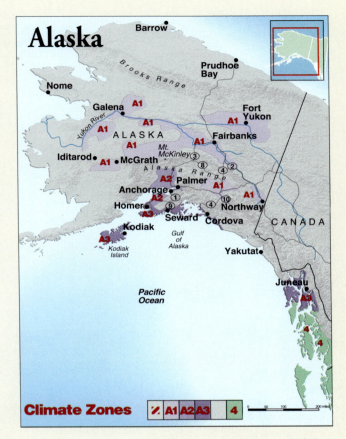

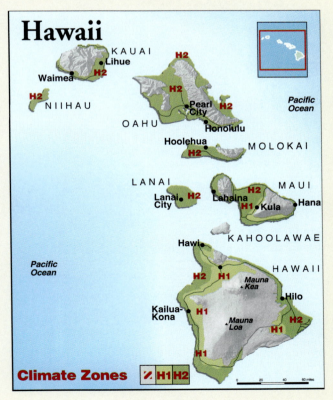

Sunset's Garden Climate Zones